KV-202-984

improving
business
results

JOHN W. HUMBLE

Director
Urwick, Orr and Partners Limited

McGRAW-HILL
Publishing Company Limited
for
MANAGEMENT CENTRE EUROPE

Published by
McGRAW-HILL Publishing Company Limited
MAIDENHEAD · BERKSHIRE · ENGLAND

94208

International Copyright © 1967, 1968 Management Centre Europe.
No part of this book may be reproduced in any part, except for
brief quotations for review purposes, without written permission
of Management Centre Europe, Brussels.

PRINTED AND BOUND IN GREAT BRITAIN

ACKNOWLEDGEMENTS

I acknowledge gratefully:

— the experience and interest of our clients, particularly K.L.M. Royal Dutch Airlines, Laporte Industries Ltd., and Smiths Industries Ltd. who have prepared case histories;

— the generous contribution of my colleagues in Urwick, Orr & Partners Ltd., particularly Ray Baker and Peter Hives in the field of Improving Management Performance, and Ken Lander for advice on Long Range Planning. I have also drawn freely on the ideas of my Associates Peter Bridgman of Urwick, Diebold Ltd., London; Pat Irwin of Urwick, Currie Ltd., Montreal; Charles Granger of Wm. E. Hill & Co. Inc., New York;

— the guidance of Bruce Recker, Managing Director, and his team at Management Centre Europe, Brussels;

— the authors and their publishers who have agreed to have their work quoted;

— the encouragement of my wife, without which the book could never have been written.

John Humble.

CONTENTS

5

PART FIVE

WIDER IMPLICATIONS

PART SIX

THE PRACTICAL EXPERIENCE OF THREE COMPANIES

APPENDIX I

SETTING COMPANY OBJECTIVES:
BASIC FACTS: A CHECK LIST

APPENDIX II

SETTING COMPANY OBJECTIVES:
INTERPRETATION: A CHECK LIST

PART ONE

AN
OVERALL VIEW
OF
IMPROVING BUSINESS
RESULTS

I. DEFINITION

IMPROVING BUSINESS RESULTS is a positive approach to improving company profit and growth through the efforts of a competent and purposeful management team.

It helps the Chief Executive to find practical answers to such questions as:

— Are our company objectives and operational plans soundly based and realistic so that we can reach our long term goals whilst *improving profitability from present operations?*

— Do subsidiary divisions, units and individual managers *clearly understand what they must do* to implement these plans?

— Are they *allowing precious high quality resources to drift into low opportunity areas?* Are they working hard to improve things which are in fact marginal or should not exist at all?

— Is our management team *highly motivated and personally committed* to reaching its objectives? Has it the necessary knowledge and skills?

— What kind of business do we plan to have in the future? Considering outside threats and opportunities and our own strengths and weaknesses from what new *earning sources will we get new profits?*

Persistent attack is required to answer such complex and fundamental questions, yet companies are still looking for a single, simple technique.

One large business set up a Strategic Planning team, staffed by expert economists, which produced a blue print full of worthwhile possibilities for the company's future. It was never put into action because, as they complain, "We couldn't sell it to senior executive management who were preoccupied with current crises". In the Sales Division of another company a Regional Manager attended a course on new developments in the social sciences. He learnt methods by which his managers and subordinates could set themselves improvement targets, and when he introduced the methods into his Region he was impressed by the response and benefits. He gave most of his time to the detail of this work and overlooked a significant change which developed in the market pattern. His competitors made an imaginative alteration in pricing policy and increased their share of the market dramatically.

In contrast, Improving Business Results requires a company to undertake the following searching work:

1. Setting Company Objectives.

The company's long and short term objectives are defined after a critical analysis of the present internal strengths and weaknesses, the threats and opportunities arising from the external environment and the expectations of stakeholders in the business.

This analysis leads to immediate profit improvement plans and also to a Strategic Plan which seeks to optimise the Company's profit potential by the best allocation of resources to product/market opportunities. In turn, the Strategic Plan is broken down into more detailed Tactical Plans with appropriate methods of reviewing actual results against expectations.

2. Improving Management Performance.

Against this background of company plans, the operating and functional units clarify their objectives. Each manager is helped to determine what he is expected to achieve by analysing his key tasks and performance standards. Managers are personally involved in all this work and are motivated, trained and developed to perform better.

It is a continuous process:

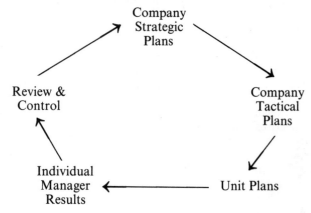

Throughout the world there is a rapid growth in interest in this subject. Although the future is uncertain as markets and technology change at an accelerating pace it is recognised that some attempt to plan ahead is essential, otherwise a company always reacts and never anticipates. There is also frustration in companies which have built up sound plans and found that implementation has been impossible because managers are indifferent or incompetent. National governments are setting a lead, no matter how imperfectly. In Britain, for example, the launching of a National Plan supported by a network of National and Industry Economic Development Committees has stirred wider discussion on long range planning in spite of the Plan's inadequacies. The planning, programming and budgeting work developed by the United States Department of Defense has been so successful that it is to be extended to another 21 departments.

However, the real driving force behind the increased number of Improving Business Results programmes comes from business pressures. For example when profits are being squeezed; the market share is declining; there is a vulnerable takeover position due to excessive cash accumulation; there is a shortage of managers for succession.

The personal involvement of the Chief Executive is essential, for he must lead the critical study of the company's present position and its long term plans and in so doing regard managers not as machines to be "programmed" but as creative people with their own views, ambitions and contribution. In this way the company plans are enriched and managers are willingly committed to success.

As their capacity to control themselves, rather than to be tightly controlled by others improves, the business becomes dynamic and flexible in its response to the outside environment. It is easier to write about the Chief Executive's involvement than to achieve it in practice. All too often glossy reports, plans and new departments are a facade of "new thinking" which is really only superficially accepted whilst the "real" job of running the business continues as before.

It is particularly difficult to put life into the mechanics and forms and infuse a business with defined purpose which really *does* change attitudes and provoke action, when it is already a "going concern" and achieving reasonable results. Without the impetus of a pressing crisis only the best Chief Executives succeed in initiating radical change in such a concern. As Selznick comments (1):

"... with many forces working to keep it (the going concern) alive, the people who run it can readily escape the task of defining its purpose. This evasion stems partly from the hard intellectual labour involved, a labour that seems but to increase the burden of already onerous daily operations. In part, also, there is the wish to avoid conflicts with those in and out of the organisation who would be threatened by a sharp definition of purpose, with its attendant claims and responsibilities."

II. THE BENEFITS

To launch Improving Business Results is demanding in terms of senior manager time and resources. Those companies which have made this investment have found such benefits as:

1. A disciplined approach to profit growth.

The need for a disciplined approach is not something to take for granted. Many of the world's great businesses have been shaped by individuals with an entrepreneurial vision, personal involvement in success and the drive and ability to get results. Men such as Henry Ford of the Ford Motor Company required no corporate planning department. Unfortunately such men are rare, and often make their unique contribution at the formative stage of a business. At the next phase of company growth it is helpful to strengthen intuition with a more systematic examination of alternative courses of action. Improvement and progress is achieved by businesses which are constantly probing their strengths and weaknesses, critically asking questions such as "what kind of business are we really in?", testing themselves against the outside environment, setting targets for better results without trying to be perfectionist. This attitude of mind is likely to unearth fundamental difficulties. For example: "No matter how we improve our present operations it becomes clear that merger, acquisition or divestment are also required if we are to generate new earnings and profit on the scale our shareholders require for the future."

Certainly, companies which do not have this self-critical attitude are in real danger as competition builds up. In the United States the classic warning is the Hollywood film business which, as T. Levitt comments (2):

"... barely escaped being ravished by television. Eventually all the established film companies went through drastic reorganisations. Some simply disappeared. All of them got into trouble not because of TV's inroads but because of their own myopia. As with the railroads, Hollywood defined its business incorrectly. It thought it was in the movie business when it was actually in the entertainment business. Movies implied a specific, limited product. This produced the fatuous contentment which from the beginning led producers to view TV as a threat. Hollywood scorned and rejected TV when it should have welcomed it as an opportunity—an opportunity to expand the entertainment business."

A recent study (3) was made of 47 firms in six industries broadly representative of British industry as a whole, in order to identify the attitudes and practices associated with high, sustained growth. The 'Thruster' companies defined their future in specific medium and long term objectives, measuring their growth in such terms as profits, assets, turnover and so on. The 'Sleepers' dealt with their problems on a day-to-day basis.

2. A more realistic balance between long and short term objectives.

Short term action can sometimes injure the vital future. When times are good some companies over-extend their investment in activities such as R and D, and management training. When there is a profit set back there is a violent swing in the opposite direction: "10% off all overhead costs." "No more people to go on outside training courses." "Cut R and D costs by 50,000 dollars" and so on.

Improving Business Results helps by providing an up to date broad framework of purpose through the Long Range Plan which has a steadying, balancing effect on "crash" programmes. It also identifies where improvements can be made and generates practical action to achieve desired results.

3. *A better capacity for dealing with business change.*

The only thing new about change is its accelerating rate. Businesses which only follow their traditional and so far successful strategies and methods are likely to be threatened. Product innovation, for example, is a vital tool in competition and will become more so as the immense increase in R and D expenditure in the last decade spawns new materials and methods. The threat of technical obsolescence is real.

Changes in business environment are equally dramatic. Channels of distribution, consumer buying habits, preference and taste are all in a state of flux, and government intervention, not always obvious, calls for sensitive judgement and timing by businessmen. For large groups the business horizon is constantly widening and becoming more international—consider the impact on European business of the large scale expansion there of American companies in the post-war years.

To predict exactly what changes will occur and to plan one's business accordingly is an ideal which can never be realised. Some companies abdicate and respond to pressures only when they are painfully felt. They regard change as a constant threat. Other companies try to anticipate change by careful study, for example of new technological developments. They recognise that the characteristics of a good long range plan include the identification of the limits of knowledge and areas of uncertainty. There is less danger of them being taken by surprise, and with a flexible and responsive organisation they are in a stronger position to avoid trouble and to exploit new opportunities.

4. *Better use of managerial resources.*

Many companies make these complaints:

> "Our managers are rather apathetic and just seem to get by without any real enthusiasm"

> "We cannot fill the tough general management jobs"

> "Our foremen won't accept responsibility"

> "There's a shortage of creative people"

14

There are complex reasons why managers, who are a vital business resource, are so wastefully used. Very often they are not at all clear what job they are expected to do, and many of the tools of management seem in practice to be weapons used against them.

A programme of Improving Business Results, properly introduced, can transform this scene. It puts into perspective the narrow and sectional goals which can encourage a partisan, selfish attitude: "As long as I get my results I'm in the clear." It becomes evident that team as well as personal objectives are required if the total business is to succeed. It proves that without the challenge and sense of purpose provided by demanding company objectives, management development has no real meaning. Where the two are blended together the impact can be remarkable and we begin to see, in Robert H. Schaffer's words (4):

"... the power of imaginative, clear cut and inspiring goals to evoke extraordinary performance from people—*and* the power of these goals to help groups merge efforts and produce joint results which transcend the simple sum of their individual capacities."

5. *Short term improvements.*

The long term changes are usually those which are really critical for the company's survival and growth. However, it is unrealistic to expect managers who are under heavy pressure now to ignore immediate profitability. In any case it is quite wrong to have an "ivory tower" study of the future. Throughout all the analyses and investigations, particularly in the process of getting all the managers to analyse for themselves where the company is strong and weak, there should be an insistent requirement that short term improvement possibilities are identified. The scope for these is very great indeed in most businesses and offer substantial financial benefits. These benefits are secured by managers motivated and trained to:

— analyse the present situation;

— look for improvement areas

— get on in a practical way with the things *they* can do and pass up the line the things which require top management approval and contribution;

— check up to see that improvements are secured.

2

An example (5) of the changes which are possible is a Manufacturing Unit employing some 700 people where "a scheme of statistical quality control was introduced, reducing the number of inspectors required by 20; a machine loading system was begun which made most of the subcontracting unnecessary; a new work measurement system was implemented, giving an initial improvement in productivity of 9 per cent with more expected later."

This work brings better profits whilst creating a climate of opinion in which the long range plans will ultimately be welcomed and put into effect, not resisted.

We will now consider the practical problems of Setting Company Objectives and then deal with the difficulties of achieving them through competent managers.

PART TWO

SETTING
COMPANY
OBJECTIVES

I. RECOGNISING THE NEED

Every company has objectives. They are usually expressed formally in profit and sales forecasts, production targets, research budgets and so on. Sometimes important objectives are implicit in the conduct of a business, for example where the owner limits its potential growth because he wishes to retain personal control.

It is always stimulating and constructive to look afresh and critically at the company's forward plans, particularly as the range of objectives is often found to be dangerously restricted. For example, a motor car manufacturer established far sighted programmes for markets, technical development, production and finance at the end of the Second World War. Little attention was paid to improving industrial relations, and plans in this field were superficial. In recent years the company has suffered a series of major strikes which has led to a "crash programme" for changing the wage structure and negotiating pattern. Failure to think through what was apparently a "secondary objective" has bitten deeply into profits. Another common defect in company objectives is their short time span, and it is not unusual to find that companies plan no more than one year ahead.

A broad framework of company objectives for say the next four or five years is of great value even though it is difficult to create. It gives a sense of corporate purpose which minimises the parochialism of functions and divisions, and it provides criteria for judging the worthwhileness of short term actions.

One way to make a start is for the Chief Executive to ask his immediate subordinates—the senior executive and functional managers—to answer individually such questions as:

— What business are we really in? What is our distinctive competence?

— Who are our customers? Who really governs the final decision to buy?

— What return are we getting on our assets? How does it compare with our competitors? What should it be five years from now to satisfy our shareholders?

— What problems in our business are so critical today that failure to solve them could jeopardise our future? What plans do we have to solve them?

— What are the significant opportunities we should be exploiting much more vigorously? What plans do we have to exploit them?
— What kind of business—in size, markets, products, physical facilities and so on—do you think we will have in five years' time?

The questions are meant to be provocative, not comprehensive. When the answers are discussed together by the top management team there will be a quick assessment of the degree of common purpose and understanding which exists.

Most companies find this simple exercise salutary. Certainly in Europe it is mainly amongst the large corporations and nationalised industries, particularly those which are capital intensive, where long range planning has been used systematically. Faced with many immediate problems, it is always easy for companies to defer a thorough consideration of forward plans. There is a deep rooted fear that since the future is uncertain, valuable time and effort put into a long range plan will only produce an academic blue-print of no practical value. The anticipated amount of preliminary work and the probability of controversial issues arising add further discouragement. Against these doubts must be set the certainty that where purpose is not clearly defined, the efforts of the company overall and of the individual managers within it, are often dissipated on trivial and non-profit influencing tasks. Moreover, complacency needs to be shaken from time to time by a disciplined and searching self analysis. As Charles Granger stresses in his article on "The Hierarchy of Objectives", (6): even a *small* amount of clarification can greatly increase the effectiveness of a business. He says objectives:

'... need not begin with the broad grand design of the enterprise, but all objectives in the hierarchy should be consistent with it.'

'... should make the people in the enterprise reach a bit.'

'... should be realistic in terms of (a) the internal resources of the enterprise, and (b) the external opportunities, threats and constraints.'

18

'... should take into account the creative conception of a range of alternatives and the relative effectiveness and cost of each.'

'... should be known to each person so that he understands the goals of his own work and how they relate to the broader objectives of the total enterprise.'

'... should be periodically reconsidered and redefined, not only to take account of changing conditions, but for the salutary effect of re-thinking the aims of organization activities.'

II. THE COMPANY PLANNING PROCESS

The Company's overall strategy for the future is summarised in its Strategic Plan which can be developed effectively by:

— assessment of company strengths and weaknesses;
— assessment of the external environment;
— consideration of the expectations of company stakeholders;
— clarification of company objectives;
— evaluation of alternative courses of action to achieve these objectives;
— development of the Strategic Plan.

The assessment and preliminary work should highlight present weaknesses and thus lead to an immediate plan for increasing profitability which need not wait until the total Strategic Plan is complete. The Strategic Plan must be converted into a series of more detailed Tactical Plans and finally into specific objectives for the units, functions and individual managers in the business.

As illustrated in Exhibit 1, company planning is a continuous process, not a 'on-off' job. After the various Plans are launched, relevant and timely information must feed back to those who are responsible so that they can take corrective action. Overall progress reviews are necessary so that plans can be revised where circumstances have changed radically. Managers will, of course, be concerned with exceptions to the planned situation and not get bogged down in detail.

* In a very large Group of companies each Division is asked to

EXHIBIT 1

COMPANY PLANNING: A CONTINUING PROCESS

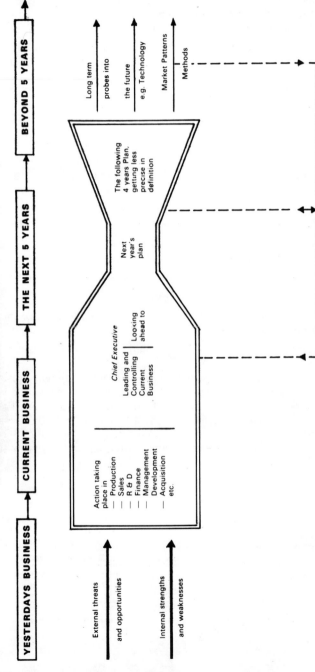

| YESTERDAYS BUSINESS | CURRENT BUSINESS | THE NEXT 5 YEARS | BEYOND 5 YEARS |

External threats and opportunities

Internal strengths and weaknesses

Action taking place in
— Production
— Sales
— R & D
— Finance
— Management
— Development
— Acquisition
etc.

Chief Executive

Leading and Controlling Current Business | Looking ahead to

Next year's plan

The following 4 years Plan, getting less precise in definition

Long term probes into the future e.g. Technology

Market Patterns

Methods

Feedback of results and findings

prepare annually a detailed Plan for the next year and a less thorough indication of their forecasts for the following four years. These Divisional Plans are built up with the active contribution of their factories, sales forces and functional advisers. Typically the Annual Plan might cover

— *Specific objectives* under such headings as profitability; sales forecasts; production forecasts; new projects for research; manager development, including succession and training; organisational changes, etc.
— Supporting these objectives would be succinct statements of *basic assumptions* on the economic, political, competitive and technology trends. For example, "Britain will not enter the European Common Market before 1972".
— Outstanding major *problems/opportunities* would be stated with Divisional Action Plans to deal with them.
— A *financial summary* of the Division Plan together with specific key performance ratios and indicators would be prepared.

These Division Plans are then reviewed centrally by an Executive Committee of the Board with advice from Group H.Q. specialists. The Division Managing Director would be involved in this review and the Plan is often revised when it has been tested in this way.

Finally, with the addition of objectives established for Central Departments, a total Group picture can be built up. Wider criteria are used to evaluate this summary: does the general shape of capital investment fit in with corporate strategy? even though each Division Plan in itself appears sound, is the balance wrong? are Divisions setting themselves overambitious goals? or do they need shaking up to reach higher standards? This stage of analysis and revision is important if the Group view is not merely to be the summary of Division views. Once the Plans are approved, Divisions get on with the job. Each month they prepare an Operating Report in which special attention is paid to financial and other key performance indicators. The basis of comparison is against the agreed objectives, *not* what was done last year, although this information also may be included in order to identify trends. The Report is discussed with and approved by the Main Board Director responsible for the Division and any major variances are raised at the Executive Committee of the Board. Four times a year a broader Report is also prepared by the Division to report progress on important but less easy to measure matters. Each year end, a thorough review is made as a preliminary to defining the following year's plan.

A small company has to think in the same terms, but the degree of paperwork and formality is obviously much reduced. The small company owner/manager has the advantage of seeing the relationship between objectives and resources more clearly and is usually in touch with problems when they arise. His disadvantage may be that in trying to keep all the knowledge in his own head he is living from crisis to crisis, too pre-occupied to look to the future. Unless he has taken advice he may miss a significant performance indicator and, for example, many small businesses collapse through over trading because their financial controls are badly designed or non existent. The small company should give itself the simple discipline of setting out next year's objectives, assumptions, problems and priorities and an outline of the following year. The second opinion of an experienced outside Board member, or professional guidance from a banker, consultant, lawyer, or accountant is often valuable when the owner has made out his first draft Plan.

The effectiveness of management control and continuity of attack in this work can be helped by three administrative devices: policies, procedures and budgets.

Policies are guides to making decisions which are in keeping with the company's overall viewpoint. They can be regarded as general laws to be interpreted by people and not specific and detailed orders or instructions. These policy guidelines in matters where questions often recur greatly facilitate understanding and speed of decision.

Procedures are much more specific rules which indicate how repetitive administrative matters must be processed so that everyone in the company is following the same pattern. It would be foolish, for example, to have each division sending in requests for capital expenditure on a different form, with different definitions of terms. On the other hand, the abuse of procedures should be recognised. Bureaucratic institutions where most decisions are made by reference to a large "Standard Procedures" volume are symbols of the way in which the proliferation of procedures can curtail management vitality.

22

Financial budgets and statements of objectives are complementary to each other, not substitutes. A financial budget itself is *not* an objective since it is merely the expression in money terms of a plan to reach certain objectives. Objectives which are intimately linked with financial budgeting are greatly strengthened. Money provides a universal measure of the worth of objectives, facilitating comparison and control, and focussing attention on the important fact that the end-product is a profitable business.

III. A THREE STEP APPROACH

Assuming a Chief Executive and his colleagues decide to clarify Company Objectives, what should they do next? There is no single answer since so much depends on the company history, operating position and personalities. Part Four of this book, "Launching an Improving Business Results Programme", deals with some factors to be considered and different sequences which pay off. It might be necessary to start at unit rather than company level and to do some preliminary work in Improving Management Performance. On the other hand, the company may be faced with a serious crisis which requires urgent decision about its total strategy. The three step approach which is now described illustrates the general questions and difficulties to be faced in setting Company objectives. It is meant to provoke thought and does not attempt to be comprehensive in scope or specific about the techniques used.

The three steps are:

    A. COLLECT BASIC FACTS.
    B. INTERPRET FACTS WHILST IMPROVING SHORT TERM PROFITABILITY.
    C. CLARIFY COMPANY OBJECTIVES.

A. COLLECT BASIC FACTS.

The collection of basic facts about the company and the environment in which it lives is an essential foundation. This either confirms that adequate knowledge already exists in the company in one form or another—in which case the work takes little time—or it shows that in important business areas unsatisfactory data is available. The need for further studies is identified and the people concerned are motivated to make them. It is impossible to build up a meaningful profile of company strengths and weaknesses unless senior management work from a common set of facts.

It is unwise to be too detailed and pedantic at the first attempt or the job is never completed. Time spent in determining the important questions to answer, before trying to answer them is always fruitful! Top management at this stage wants a broad appreciation of the position which is sufficiently accurate to signal significant problem areas, trends and opportunities.

The size and sophistication of the company will suggest who should be responsible for collecting this information. One large trading group set up a Working Party led by the Managing Director with a senior marketing executive appointed full time as Company Long Range Planner. A manufacturing company employing five hundred people did most of the detailed work directly in the operating departments concerned, with the Company Secretary acting as part time co-ordinator. Whatever methods suit a company there are important common requirements:

— The Chief Executive must be involved personally with his most senior people in defining the questions and interpreting the answers.

— The contribution of a wide cross section of managers in the business must be secured so that their up-to-date and practical views are included and their interest stimulated in the study and its outcome.

— The Long Range Planner or Co-ordinator—the person directly responsible for the collation and analysis—must be a person of high calibre. This is not a "fill-in" job for the new graduate trainee...

— A programme, setting out the stages of work and completion date, must be agreed and kept to or the study will constantly be postponed by the pressure of current crises.

— Creating additional paperwork must be avoided as far as possible. For example, sound existing data may not be available in the form the original question requires. Unless

24

there are convincing reasons to the contrary the question should be rephrased. Similarly, where the work involved in collecting new facts is large the Long Range Planning Group should be consulted to see if the data really is vital; or whether a decision on the need for it can be postponed until the general company picture becomes clearer.

Each company must work out its own list of information required but Appendix I suggests typical questions in areas such as:

— Company Performance and Finance.

— External environment.

— Product/market position.

— Physical resources.

— Innovation.

— Organisation and manager development.

— Worker performance.

B. INTERPRET FACTS WHILST IMPROVING SHORT TERM PROFITABILITY.

The effort of collecting facts is completely wasted unless profitable action follows. In practice, no clear division can be drawn between collecting facts, interpreting them, finding glaring defects which *must* be corrected, identifying improvement opportunities which *must* be grasped, becoming aware of the need for more facts and beginning to shape crude models for the future. The time span and priority of different issues which are identified require different treatment. This merging of effort, strongly oriented to taking practical action, is vital and healthy although some discipline is required if one is to avoid the Stephen Leacock situation of "jumping on a horse and riding off in all directions at the same time".

1. Attitudes to interpretation.

The leadership of the Chief Executive is particularly important when the facts are interpreted and he must create a climate of opinion in which his senior team can be *completely frank* and *self critical*. If he fails to achieve this the study becomes a façade.

It is not easy to bring out the truth if the prevailing attitude is "Play it safe. Don't promise anything you're not *sure* will happen or you'll be in trouble" or "Tell the President what is wrong with middle management but don't risk pointing out the confusion coming from his office".

Throughout the discussions, no one should be seeking perfection or final details, but rather taking a general management view of the scope for improvement. In businesses which have had an impressive growth and profit record, the cutting edge of self criticism can become blunted and complacency creeps in. In a famous paper, "Marketing myopia", (7), Theodore Levitt warns us that:

"Industries that assume themselves to be riding some automatic growth escalator invariably descend into stagnation. The history of every dead and dying "growth" industry shows a self-deceiving cycle of bountiful expansion and undetected decay. There are four conditions which usually guarantee this cycle:

1. The belief that growth is assured by an expanding and more affluent population.

2. The belief that there is no competitive substitute for the industry's major product.

3. Too much faith in mass production and in the advantages of rapidly declining unit costs as output rises.

4. Pre-occupation with a product that lends itself to carefully controlled scientific experimentation, improvement, and manufacturing cost reduction."

The danger of being over introspective during interpretation should also be avoided. The internal strengths and weaknesses are important but it is *with the customer outside the business where profit and opportunity really lie*. Listening to some Board discussions sometimes leaves one with the impression that the customer is regarded only as the means by which products that are going to be made anyway, will finally be converted into cash!

Two other recurring themes justify special attention. First, the *gross misallocation of high quality resources* to low quality opportunities. For example, a factory in an engineering business commonly lost money, its product had little future and "one

26

day" the factory would be closed. The ablest production manager was assigned to this factory in order to reduce losses. Meanwhile a large modern plant, making products with high sales potential was being mismanaged by a second-rate man.

Another example (8) is Courtaulds Ltd. which a few years ago decided that its fundamental research laboratory was doing work for which the commercial utility was remote. The laboratory was closed and the researchers transferred to applied research. This concentration on improving its basic business —viscose rayon—has produced a range of developments which have made rayon a growth product again. The second theme is aptly summarised by a Company President who said "*We're using a shot gun instead of a rifle*" when he looked critically at the product range and found 83% of the profit coming from 30% of the lines. He also found that the management control system recently introduced provided new and interesting data but missed some of the vital profit matters middle managers were trying to control.

2. The questions to ask.

Some typical questions are shown in Appendix II, but of course each company must decide for itself which questions are important.

3. The practical outcome.

Three things should come from the interpretation:

First: Immediate plans to improve profitability.
If the work so far has not identified worthwhile areas where improvement can be made in the short term then it has been badly done. Every business that honestly is self critical discovers such opportunities. Perhaps they should *sell more* of their present main product by making price changes and arranging better service? Maybe the sales force organisation and commission payments need revision? Or the attack may be on *cost reduction* through product standardisation and simplification; or a reduction in material costs through value analysis and scrap control. Important opportunities might lie in *reduced investment,*

27

such as reductions in the work in progress levels. A co-ordinated Improvement Plan for the major opportunities can be established and implemented by making clear to each manager his personal responsibility for securing specific results, to an agreed standard, within a time limit and by setting up a control and review method. An effective way to do this will be illustrated in Part 3 of this book, "Improving Management Performance".

A determined attack on these short term problems and opportunities is very important. The Strategic Plan will take many months to develop and there is no reason why immediate gains should not be made within the present business framework. These gains can be significant:

— An English engineering company improved the effectiveness of delivery service from 35% to 75% in six months.

— A Brazilian pesticide/fertiliser group changed its selling organisation, set up a new market research department and introduced more effective credit controls.

— A South African gold mine introduced a new type of organisation structure for underground operations, with associated improved controls over labour and materials.

— An English chemical plant put its major Improvement Plan effort into the Engineering Department. In the first 9 months, shutdown hours due to engineering causes were reduced by 58%; maintenance manhours per ton produced were reduced by 11.2%; design costs were controlled to within 5.1% of total project costs, a reduction of .8%.

The non-financial benefits are also valuable. Many managers who co-operated with the fact-collecting may be unconvinced that any action will follow. For them it was probably an extra burden put on by Headquarters. Once they are involved in specific action plans to solve some of the problems, there is a transformation in motivation and attitude. Moreover, until managers are helped to concentrate on fewer, really important issues, and some improvement made in persistent difficulties which cause crises, it is unrealistic to ask them to find time to think about the future.

Second: Important gaps in knowledge.
The second outcome is recognition that in some key business areas there is not adequate information. This can lead to further

studies. For example, a company troubled by high labour turnover in its workforce investigated the earnings and conditions of employment offered by local firms competing with them for labour. A small wool textile spinning mill found it necessary to take professional advice from a specialist accountant in order to distinguish the profit made from timely purchase of wool tops—the raw material—and the actual conversion of it into spun yarn. It was discovered that the skill of the buyer was masking the ineffective running of the mill.

Further work of this kind must be commissioned only when the senior management team is convinced that the information is essential. The temptation to collect information "for general background" or because "it would be interesting" must be firmly resisted.

Third: Identification of long term problems.
At this stage some of the major problems the company must face in the next four or five years are highlighted. For example:

"Two customers provide most of our turnover: is this a dangerous situation we should alter?"

"Our high class departmental store in the city centre is losing trade to competitors who are placed in the expanding suburbs. Discount houses are attacking our consumer durable business. Although we are still a profitable business what should our long term strategy be?"

"We are convinced that Britain will enter the European Common Market in the next five years. The impact on our traditional price and sales structure will be significant but so far we have done no systematic work to prepare ourselves."

C. CLARIFY COMPANY OBJECTIVES.

It is now possible to restate the objectives of the company and to begin to clarify them although it would be naive to suggest that they could be precise and final as yet. The real justification for a disciplined and formal statement is that it stimulates action for improvement, no matter how imperfect are the initial objectives.

3

1. Profitability: the "single objective" view.

A business which does not use profitability as the final test of its effectiveness may find that it has not earned enough to replace its plant, or that it cannot attract in capital when this is required. However, the definition of objectives in *all* the key result areas in a business is essential because the objective "to make a profit" is a platitude without supporting action plans to secure it. As every manager knows, it is easy to maximise short term profit by neglecting things such as plant replacement, manager development and research which may in the long term be of great importance for business survival. Another argument advanced in support of the single "profitability" objective is that many of the secondary objectives are unreliable: they reflect compromise amongst influential people; they are subjective and governed by personal goals; they are based on doubtful factual premises. The conclusion is that it is more realistic to leave them in very general terms. This argument certainly has more validity when the first two steps we have described have not been done thoroughly.

Igor Ansoff, in his book on "Corporate Strategy" puts these views into practical perspective when he sums up his system of objectives thus:

"1. The firm has both (a) "economic" objectives aimed at optimizing the efficiency of its total resource conversion process and (b) "social" or non-economic objectives, which are the result of interaction among individual objectives of the firm's participants.

2. In most firms the economic objectives exert the primary influence on the firm's behaviour and form the main body of explicit goals used by management for guidance and control of the firm.

3. *The central purpose of the firm is to maximise long-term return on resources employed within the firm.*

4. The social objectives exert a secondary, modifying and constraining influence on management behaviour.

5. In addition to proper objectives two related types of influence are exerted on management behaviour: responsibilities and constraints."

30

In Ansoff's terms, responsibilities are obligations which the firm undertakes to discharge, but which do not form part of the firm's internal guidance and control mechanism. Constraints are decision rules which limit a firm's freedom of action; for example, a minimum wage level is usually a legal or contractual constraint, not an objective.

2. The range of objectives.

If the need for more than one objective is accepted then drawing on Drucker, (10), the range might be:

1. Profitability, i.e. the intention to make a return of $x\%$ on net assets of $£y$ and over the period 1967 to 1972.

2. Market standing, e.g. share of market; volume of sales; product quality and leadership; field representation; price; marketing effectiveness.

3. Productivity, e.g. improvement in ratio of output to input, such as number of units per worker or per period of time; output per measure of space or per pound of investment; sales per salesman; volume per sales call; calls per sale and so on.

4. Financial and physical resources, e.g. specific objectives for identifying, acquiring, conserving and developing the resources needed by each operating unit and function.

5. Innovation, e.g. the planned development of new and better products and processes and services; better marketing strategies; new pricing methods.

6. Manager performance and development, e.g. selection; training; succession; salary structure and benefits; promotion and succession.

7. Worker performance and attitude, e.g. specific measures to improve the motivation and contribution of workers such as progressive productivity bargains; better security and working conditions; more effective negotiations.

8. Public responsibility, e.g. attitude to membership of Economic Development Committee; financial support for local educational and cultural ventures.

3. The balance of objectives.

Finding the right balance between worthy but conflicting objectives is one of top management's most difficult jobs. Courage and old fashioned judgment and entrepreneurial flair come into their own at this stage, helped by illuminating data from the preliminary work. If too much emphasis is placed on the long term future, shareholders may become disillusioned, especially as these strategies are often more speculative. On the other hand, over pre-occupation with short term results may lead to a disaster situation where one's product becomes obsolete. Large companies—particularly in capital intensive industries—are obliged to take a long view because they do not have the flexibility to change direction quickly.

Faced with limited resources, should a company invest in new plant to exploit the lead it has in a certain product? should it instead increase investment in R and D where some even more promising products appear to be at a breakthrough stage? Is it possible—and wise—to try to do a little of each and risk doing both badly? An important justification for time spent on thinking about the overall company position and strategic aims is that it gives perspective to these questions. Top management is better equipped to see the business as a total system with dynamic interactions, not a series of unrelated problems and prospects.

The practical difficulties in achieving this unity, especially in large and complex businesses, are great and three points must be emphasised. First, since any attempt to interlock different levels of objectives in detail is bound to fail, great concentration must be made on selecting a limited number of priorities which *must* be linked from top to bottom of the business. If this is done then any contradictions will at least be confined to peripheral matters. Second, it must be recognised that the interlocking of these key objectives is not only vertical, in the direct line of command. The *cross links,* e.g. between sales and production objectives, are just as important and indeed usually cause most problems in establishing common purpose. Third, short term objectives can be regarded as intermediate destinations along a logical path to the long term objectives. Thus short and long term objectives are ideally consistent with each other always.

32

In practice, difficulties which cannot immediately be removed emerge as obstacles in the direct path to one's long term goals. Short term objectives may have to be used as a detour i.e. a longer, more costly route than the direct one, but the only practical way to arrive at all! Thus the "ideal":

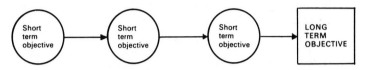

is often found to be:

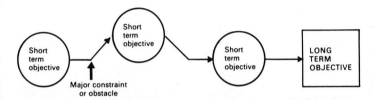

4. The hierarchy of objectives.

It is important to recognise within a business that there is a hierarchy of objectives. The mission of the business provides a very broad concept which is helpful in shaping Strategic Plans. In turn Strategic Plans must be broken down into more detailed Tactical Plans. Finally each unit, department and finally the individual managers must be clear what objectives they must reach.

We will consider these various types of objectives:

a. *Mission.* This can be described as a broad concept of the business which is conscientiously pursued. "To achieve a fair return for our stockholders through leadership in the manufacture and distribution of metal windows in the United States." This may seem too general and academic to be of value but the discussions which led to this statement caused major rethinking of company strategy. For a small family business to state explicitly its determination to remain a growth company only within the constraint of keeping personal family control is an essential guideline for long range

EXHIBIT 2

DEVELOPING THE STRATEGIC PLAN [11]

1. **MARKETS**

   A. FACTORS AFFECTING PRODUCT-MARKETS

      1. Economic
      2. Sociological
      3. Technological
      4. Political

   B. PRODUCT-MARKET STRATEGIES

	Current Product	New Product
Present Market	Market Penetration	Product Development
New Market	Market Development	Diversification

2. **COMPETITION**

   A. FOR CUSTOMERS

      1. Performance in selected markets
      2. Other ways of satisfying needs

   B. FOR RESOURCES

      1. Finance
      2. Personnel
      3. Material
      4. Other

ASSESS EXTERNAL ENVIRONMENT

ASSESS COMPANY PERFORMANCE, STRENGTH AND LIMITATIONS

Business(es)
Profitability

CLARIFY COMPANY OBJECTIVES

Innovation
Market Standing
Productivity
Financial & Physical Resources
Manager Performance & Development
Worker Performance & Attitude
Public Responsibility

ASSESS EXPECTATIONS OF COMPANY'S STAKEHOLDERS

Owners
Employees
Customers

PLANS TO INCREASE IMMEDIATE PROFITABILITY

EVALUATE ALTERNATIVE COURSES OF ACTION TO ACHIEVE OBJECTIVES

The strategic plan

action plans. The plans would be quite different if the family stated that they wished to "Maximise short term, not long term profitability in order to sell the business within the next X years at not less than £ Y".

b. *Strategic Plan.* The Strategic Plan (Exhibit 2) looks ahead at the way in which resources should be redeployed to optimise market and product opportunities. So far, the initial studies may have led to making the present business more profitable in the short term. Strategic considerations may make it clear that no matter how the *present* business is improved there are fundamental constraints which will prevent it from providing stockholders with a fair return ten years from now. A long term view is obviously made uncertain by the accelerating pace of technical, political and social change. The stimulus to improvement and better understanding amongst the senior management alone should justify the work. It is also helpful to have a written statement of intention and assumptions to go back to and revise, when things do not work out as anticipated. At *least* the preparation of a Strategic Plan is educational and a discipline for clear thinking! If this modest claim seems unsatisfactory the alternative courses are even more so. Merely taking a "year-by-year view" means that the company is always reacting to pressure and not anticipating it. To rely on one man's entrepreneurial vision to shape the company's profitable growth may leave a dangerous position when he retires or dies.

The facts, interpretation and critical insight brought to bear at earlier stages merge imperceptibly into discussion of alternatives and finally the draft Strategic Plan. The company is looking for major trends, perception into the relationships between known facts and the scope for fundamental change in the business pattern. These questions might be asked:

What are the important opportunities and threats?

Have we really planned to get all the profit we can from our present business?

Is there a 'profit gap'—see Exhibit 3—which must be filled by merger, acquisition or new products? Is there a major technological breakthrough which will affect our products? Can we deal with the necessary developments through our own R and D or should we try to 'buy in' know-how?

35

What must we do to minimise seasonal and cyclical fluctuations?

Are there constraints we cannot alter?

What are our basic assumptions for the next 5 years?

e.g. "Britain will not be engaged in a major war."

"Defence spending in the U.S.A. will be maintained at least at present levels."

"The main source of our raw material will become increasingly unreliable through political strife in the supplying countries."

"The movement of population to settle in the S.E. of England will continue."

What is the state of our resources?

Is our financial structure and current situation such that we have flexibility to manœuvre?

Do our physical resources such as plant and factories form an efficient and complementary resource in line with the market opportunities? Or do we have to face the fact that the past pattern of capital investment has left us a legacy of out-of-date, haphazardly linked units?

What strengths do we have in our management team? Is there depth to our managerial talent? In what areas do we have people of outstanding knowledge and skills? Are these human assets in line with likely market/product demands?

Is our business decentralised into profit centres where we can build in an effective management by objectives approach?

What is our distinctive competence as a business?

Can we identify the secret of our past success?

Why do our customers come to us not our competitors?

What do we want to do?

What are the wishes and expectations of stakeholders in the business?

What degree of risk are they prepared to take?

What should be our product/market strategy?

For example, should we develop

— Current products in present markets (Market penetration).

THE PROFIT GAP

EXHIBIT 3

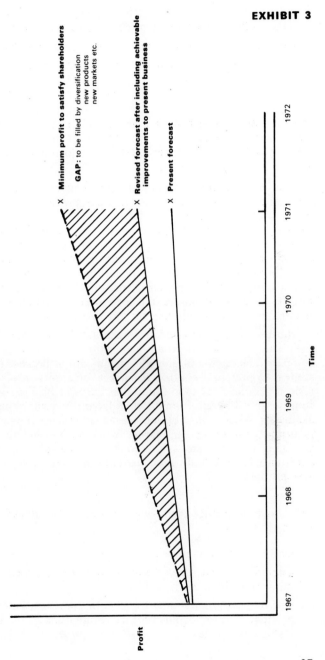

X Minimum profit to satisfy shareholders

GAP: to be filled by diversification
new products
new markets etc.

X Revised forecast after including achievable
improvements to present business

X Present forecast

Profit

Time

1967   1968   1969   1970   1971   1972

— New products in present markets (Product Development).

— Current products in new markets (Market Development).

— New products in new markets (Diversification).

Two cases.

These questions are general and incomplete since the pattern varies with every situation, but they are all profoundly difficult to answer. Take the question of "distinctive competence".

* One paper making group thought that their special strength lay in the management of complex process industries and associated research. Since they wanted to diversify, it seemed logical to look for opportunities where these strengths could be used, for example, chemicals or plastics. Outside advisers diagnosed that in process management and research the company *was* good, but not better than many others. Its special competence lay in a superb national sales force calling directly on retail outlets and much greater growth and profit opportunities lay in building on this distribution network.

* Another case is reported by Mace and Montgomery in their study (12) of corporate acquisitions: "A basic resin company... bought a plastic boat manufacturer because this seemed to present a controlled market for a portion of the resin it produced. It soon found that the boat business was considerably different from the manufacture and sale of basic chemicals. After a short but unpleasant experience in manufacturing and trying to market what was essentially a consumer's item, the management concluded that its experience lay essentially in industrial rather than consumer-type products."

The final Strategic Plan will include clear objectives relating to:

— The selected business(es).

— The selected markets, products and services, and the required share of each market.

— The return on investment for each business, market and product, and the detailed objectives for each of the key result areas.

— Decisions on divestment of non-profitable activities or activities which no longer fit the planned shape of the business.

— Decisions on diversification through:
a. Research and development or
b. Mergers or acquisitions, or both.

— The allocation of resources to each element of strategy and a timetable for results.

Here are some examples of strategic objectives extracted from a number of company statements:

"To increase earnings from 4 dollars U.S. per share in 1964 to 6 dollars U.S. per share in 1974."

"To ensure within four years that no one market accounts for more than 50% of the output; no one customer accounts for more than 25% of the output; and no one product accounts for more than $12\frac{1}{2}\%$ of the output."

"To increase our share of the United Kingdom market for product XYZ from 1963 12% to 1969 21%."

"To increase output per hour of manufacturing labour by 2% per annum."

"To turn over assets: receivables 9 times annually and inventories (raw material, work in progress, finished goods) 3 times annually within three years."

"To divest ourselves of Division PQR and its associated products by selling out to either Smith or Jones. Objective: Sale to be complete in six years."

"To establish in the European Common Market at least three production units and a sales force either by acquisition or our own resources by 1973."

"In the next five years we intend to reduce our man hours for present production levels by 35%. To achieve this we intend to spend £ 3.5 million in reconstructing our main plant and modernising another. These changes will be secured without redundancies and without going to the outside market for cash."

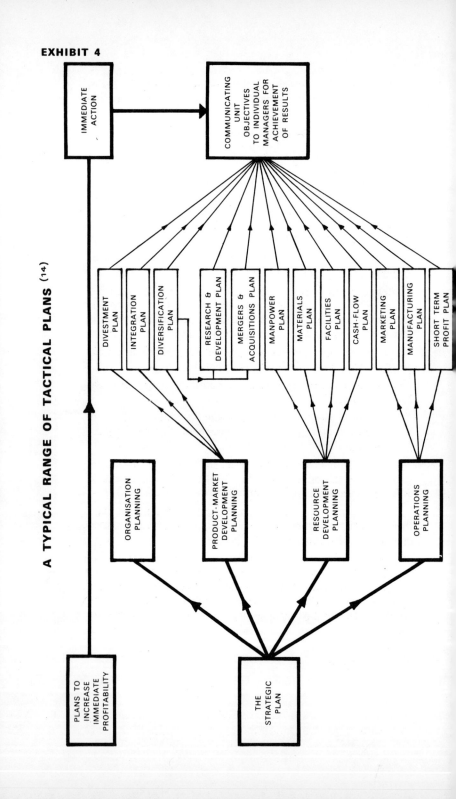

EXHIBIT 4

A TYPICAL RANGE OF TACTICAL PLANS (14)

EXHIBIT 5

SOME COMPANY OBJECTIVES AND THEIR RELATIONSHIP WITH DEPARTMENTAL AND SECTIONAL OBJECTIVES (13)

To achieve a Net Profit of 25 per cent before tax on net assets at written down value.
To increase employee earnings by 3½ per cent.
To avoid any increase in prices during the year.
To design, manufacture and market the proposed products C and D.
To increase our share of the market from 30 to 45 per cent.

Department	Section
Design To complete the design of new products C and D not later than May.	*Design Office* To complete the design studies for new products C and D not later than March.
To modify the design of products A and B to meet the requirements of Sales Report 16-11-65 not later than March.	*Drawing Office* To complete the working for new products C and D not later than May.
To reduce the variety of component parts by not less than 15 per cent.	To modify the working drawings of products A and B not later than March.
To investigate and report on the feasibility of a part number coding system by June.	To investigate the various systems of part number coding by March; carry out a feasibility study by May; and report by June.
To keep within an overhead expenditure of £20,000.	To recommend action to eliminate 15 per cent of variety of component parts by July.
Manufacturing To achieve an output of £1 m., including not less than £50,000 of new products C and D.	*Machine Shop* To achieve an output of not less than £900,000 of machined parts.
To achieve a delivery performance of not less than 95 per cent of orders delivered on time.	To meet 95 per cent of all due dates for machined parts.
To reduce standard manufacturing cycle time from 25 weeks to 15 weeks.	To reduce machined parts cycle times from 18 weeks to 11 weeks.
To maintain an average value of Work in Progress of not more than £250,000 and total stocks of not more than £500,000.	To investigate the possibility of using plug-board capstan lathes and report to Works Manager by March.
To keep within an overhead expenditure of £20,000.	To maintain an average value of Work in Progress of not more than £100,000.
	Tool Room To complete jigs, tools and fixtures for new products C and D by August.
	To introduce ceramic tooling whenever applicable.
	To rationalise stocking policy for all standard cutting tools.
Accounts To develop the accounting system to produce the monthly accounts not later than 7 days after the end of the period.	*Costing* Propose and agree timetable to achieve issue of monthly accounts at required time.
To devise quarterly Product Accounts showing profitability and return on net assets by products.	Design simplified accounting routine.
Review and revise if necessary the Accounts Coding system.	Achieve collection of data by times laid down in accounting timetable.
To keep within an overhead expenditure of £17,000.	*Financial Accounts* Revise method of producing quarterly Product Accounts.
	Review and report on Accounts coding system.

c. *Tactical Plans*. These are much more detailed, shorter term plans which are necessary to reach the strategic goals. See Exhibit 4.

Typically they would include Tactical Plans for Organisation, Product/Market Development, Resource Development and Operations.

For example, the Product/Market Development Plan could include a series of plans for divestment, integration, diversification, research, mergers and acquisitions.

They may be carried out at Company level or delegated further to units such as a factory, a sales force, a research laboratory. These plans specify the results required; the resources to be provided; the means of control and review; the date for completion.

Exhibit 5 shows examples of departmental and section objectives in the context of some of the company's one year objectives.

An example of a large corporation using a series of tactical plans to achieve its strategic goals is the Singer Manufacturing Company. The main features of a report (15) prepared by John Thackray, are:

In 1958 the great Singer company produced a return on total assets of 2.5% and a return on shareholders equity of 4%. According to the new President, Mr. Kircher, the company's past success "... had led to the assumption that all the answers were found, and that all one had to do was do what one's predecessors had done before."

"Everything got ingrained. There were no outside influences acting on the company. It became withdrawn into itself."

From his critical analysis of the position the following changes were made:

Sewing machines

— an immediate sales attack on European competition in the U.S., which virtually eliminated the competition.
— development of a new low priced "zig-zag" machine to meet Japanese competition.

42

Internal diversification

— use of Singer retail outlets to sell other consumer products. Washing machines and refrigerators now account for one sixth of total European retail sales. An Italian refrigerator company has been acquired to support this trade.

External diversification

— merger with Friden, a highly successful business machine manufacturer with 1962 sales in the order of 105.2 million dollars. This gave Singer important growth prospects away from sewing machines;

— acquisition of three small companies in the field of electronic laboratory and field test equipment and their integration into Singer Metrics;

— further small acquisitions which dovetail with the business.

Organisational change

The highly centralised functional organisation was changed into a series of decentralised profit centres. Senior managers who could not respond to the new challenges were removed: six out of the present fourteen Vice-Presidents are from outside the business.

Many mistakes were made, such as an unsuccessful attempt to distribute refrigerators and washing machines in the U.S.; an abortive attempt to set up a Defence Products Division following the acquisition of a small defence company; serious and costly labour difficulties at the large Clydebank Works through over-ambitious attempts to modernize quickly. But the Plans are steadily beginning to pay off and by 1965 the net return on shareholders investment had risen to 10.2%. Mr. Kircher plans to accelerate this improvement in the next few years by solving more of the outstanding problems within the company and by shrewd acquisition.

d. *Individual Manager Objectives.* The final link is made by tying in the unit and departmental objectives with the key results an individual manager must achieve, his standards of performance and controls. The techniques for doing this—Key Results Analysis and Job Improvement Plan—will be described and illustrated in the next part of this book.

PART THREE

IMPROVING MANAGEMENT PERFORMANCE

I. INTRODUCTION

A perceptive company's forward plan, rich with potential profit growth, is useless until managers at all levels put it into action. Their competence, judgment and enthusiasm will determine whether or not the company objectives are achieved.

At first sight this is not a difficult problem. We could

— *tell* each manager precisely what he must do;
— set up control procedures so that top management can correct the manager when there is deviation from standard;
— systematically teach managers the knowledge and skills they need.

Those who have used this method have found it helpful and a vast improvement on the uncertainty and anarchy which so often exists. Yet the long term results prove disappointing. A passive rather than a positive spirit is created and managers grow mechanistic, inflexible and somewhat dependent on their superiors. Their budgets and forecasts are cautious so that they are reasonably certain to keep out of trouble. This apparently sensible and logical approach often misses the spark of vitality, challenge and involvement on which the real use of human beings depends.

A. DEFINITION.

A different approach—Improving Management Performance— has been developed in recent years and used in over fifty companies throughout the world. They range in size from 200 to 65,000 employees and include such industries as engineering, transport, retailing, mining, food, textiles, chemicals, cutlery, building and civil engineering and local government. Essential features of Improving Management Performance are:

* Clarifying with each manager the *Key Results and Performance Standards* he must achieve, in line with *unit and company objectives,* and gaining his contribution and commitment to these.

* Agreeing with each manager a *Job Improvement Plan* which makes a measurable and realistic contribution to the unit and company's Improvement Plans.

45

* Providing conditions in which it is possible to achieve the Key Results and Improvement Plans, notably:
  — an *organisation structure* which gives managers maximum freedom and flexibility in operation;
  — *management control information* in a form and at a frequency which makes for more effective self-control and better and quicker decision making;
  — a sense of *team spirit and corporate purpose.*

* Using systematic *Performance Review* to measure and discuss progress towards results and *Potential Review* to identify men with potential for advancement.

* Developing *Management Training Plans* to help each manager to overcome his weaknesses, to build on his strengths and to accept a responsibility for self development.

* Strengthening a manager's motivation by effective *selection, salary* and *succession plans.*

From one point of view, Improving Management Performance is seen as an integral part of managing a business—see Exhibit 6. Looked at in another way it is a vital method of developing the contribution and motivation of each manager in the business—see Exhibit 7.

B. TYPICAL BENEFITS.

Typical benefits obtained include:

— concentration by individual managers and working teams, on the really important, profit influencing tasks instead of dissipating their energy on things which even if done superbly well could have little impact on overall results and growth;

— better delegation, as a manager clarifies more precisely with his subordinates the results they must achieve and uses performance review as a regular discipline for accountability;

— the identification of problems which prevent high performance, and the establishment of improvement plans to solve them. e.g. In one engineering company an analysis of the production manager's key results revealed weaknesses in process control which in turn led to a 12 per cent reduction in scrap;

46

IMPROVING MANAGEMENT PERFORMANCE
A "BUSINESS VIEW"

EXHIBIT 6

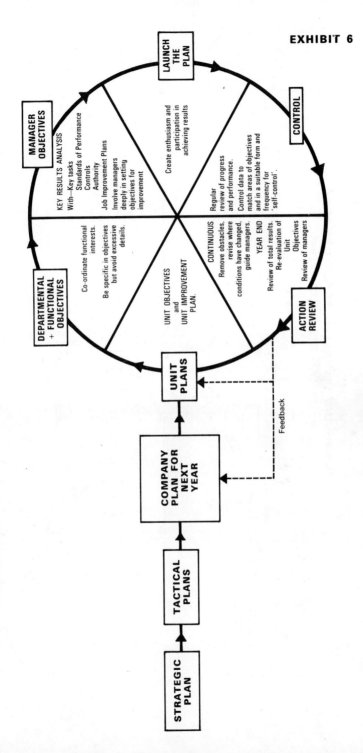

EXHIBIT 7

IMPROVING MANAGEMENT PERFORMANCE
A 'HUMAN RESOURCE' VIEW

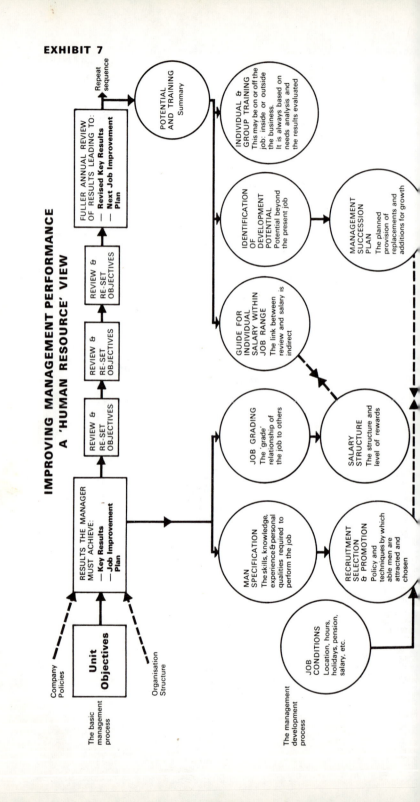

— a demonstrable improvement in morale and sense of purpose arising from the involvement of managers, and their recognition that this method is of practical value. e.g. Labour turnover amongst key staff, which arose mainly from frustration was reduced in a multiple retail concern within a year of introducing management by objectives;

— the identification of men with potential so that reliable management succession plans can be built up. e.g. A large transport business found that its management succession plan was meaningless because the technique of judging a manager's contribution to the business was defective and misleading;

— better management training at a lower cost. e.g. A critical study of management training in a consumer durable manufacturing group showed that its content was mainly what the personnel department thought was necessary and not the real needs, shown by performance review. A group of managers were being trained in 'report writing and communications' when the urgent priority was for them to understand and use a new method of statistical quality control. People were sent on outside training courses by rota with little consideration of individual problems and with no provision for follow up action on return;

— improvements in management controls. e.g. It may be much more meaningful to express control data in tons/man hours rather than money, or to provide crude evidence of trends quickly rather than wait for more accurate information. These points, to which lip service is often given, emerge vividly when controls are related to specific results which a manager agrees to achieve to a specific standard. Papers and statistics of no real management value can be discontinued.

II. MANAGEMENT DEVELOPMENT: A CRITICAL REVIEW

The management development programmes which many progressive companies introduced after the Second World War were designed to secure benefits of this kind. In spite of some progress, there is widespread recognition that early promises have not been kept and that it is now timely to review critically what has gone wrong.

49

A. BASIC FAILURES.

The failures, which are fundamental and not just defects in procedures, include:

1. Failure to integrate Management Development and Company Objectives.

It has been stressed that every business requires objectives—long and short term, financial and non-financial—and these must be established after thorough study and evaluation of the company's strengths and weaknesses and the influence of outside environment. Consistent with these objectives, sub-objectives must be established for each department or subsidiary unit.

The tragedy is that few managers really understand the company's objectives and what their own contribution should be to them. 'Grey areas' can lead to frustration, as well intentioned men strive for different and sometimes conflicting goals. It is a situation where managers are often judged on how busy they appear to be, rather than what relevant results they produce. In one company the production manager sought to increase throughput whilst maintaining quality. In fact, the forward sales position was poor and he should have been planning how to keep unit costs low with reduced throughput; how to improve on delivery dates; how to improve quality. Management development has too often been a 'separate activity' in the business, associated with the Personnel Department, and not seen as a dynamic means for executive management to link personal and company performance.

2. Stressing Personality rather than Performance.

When considering the appointment of a new Works Manager, the Production Director of a large engineering group was given staff appraisal forms for three superintendents. They were all highly rated in such terms as decision, stability, adaptability and tact. He said "They look all right on paper but I'd rather have Smith—another man—although I know he was only rated 'average'. Smith gets results". Too much effort has been

50

put into the definition of an 'ideal' manager's personality traits and not enough into judging how well he contributes to the company's success. To build an effective team we need a variety of personalities, not one stereotype endlessly repeated. A corollary of this preoccupation has been an undue emphasis on human relations training. Personality is very important, but in the work situation we are concerned primarily with the *use* a man makes of his personality to secure results.

3. *"Programmitis".*

Some companies have had too much faith in a mechanistic set of procedures, implicitly assuming that if people are appraised, sent on their quota of courses and shown in a neat square on a replacement chart all will be well. The problem has been made acute by extensive borrowing of other company procedures without any attempt to confirm that they are appropriate to the new situation. Good procedures are necessary, but they are subordinate to an analysis of a manager's work and the way in which his superior helps him improve. Douglas McGregor was right when he said (16) that we need an agricultural analogy in 'growing' talent rather than an industrial one of 'manufacturing' it.

At a deeper level, a manager has a great deal to contribute to the improvement of his job and the establishment of realistic objectives. Many management development programmes have not succeeded in securing this willing contribution. The manager must be personally involved at every stage and the whole approach should be flexible and human, not authoritarian and rigid.

4. *Crown Prince complex.*

Radical changes in the educational structure make it essential to recruit young men at varying ages and levels of academic achievement. Each intake will require special plans. However, a common mistake is to believe that management development problems are solved only by introducing a 'trainee scheme', especially when the scheme involves a year or two of watching without any weight of responsibility. A planned approach to identifying men of high potential and systematically shaping their experience is essential in every business. Such a scheme must always be supported by a planned approach to improving the performance of all managers on a continuous basis.

Too many systems have excluded the 'dark horses' and 'poor starters'. In an American General Electric study (17), researchers dug out a list of 143 'promising young men' of ten years ago, and followed up on their careers. Only 37 per cent had achieved the success predicted for them at the time of appraisal.

5. Over-emphasis on promotion.

Most management development programmes over-emphasize promotion. This influences managers to devote too much thought to the future instead of concentrating on achieving first class results on their present job.

They become frustrated because advancement never seems to come as quickly as expected.

Although promotion *is* important and a manager should be helped to enlarge his capacity and experience for a bigger job, he should earn advancement mainly by outgrowing his present job. Promotion should be a ladder, requiring effort and sacrifice to climb, not an escalator. Development is primarily a manager's own responsibility, although the company must provide stimulus and opportunity.

6. Abdication by executive management.

Specialist personnel departments have often taken staff development responsibility from managers, implying that it is too complex and specialized for 'laymen'. Line managers have often been glad to relinquish this responsibility. If the view of management development as a 'work centred' activity is accepted it follows that every manager is responsible for agreeing objectives with his staff, training them, judging their performance and encouraging them. It is a responsibility that cannot be delegated. Personnel specialists should be advisers and professional counsellors to line managers.

7. *Pursuit of fashionable techniques.*

Some companies seem to have no stability in developing their managers. They pursue each fashionable technique or idea with enthusiasm, seeing it as the panacea for all ailments.

'It's important to communicate with foremen -
let's have a newsletter and three-monthly conferences.'

'There's a new course on decision-making -
we must send all our managers on it.'

'Sensitivity training is the breakthrough we need.
After all, we have to work in groups to get things done.'

There is often genuine merit in the technique... but only if it is seen in perspective as just one part of a continuous and developing inter-relationship between objectives, personal results, review, training and wider opportunity.

8. *Management development as an 'act of faith'.*

Large sums of money have been invested by companies in management development activities. It is usually accepted that a measurable return cannot be expected from this money- "After all, education must always be an act of faith" said one Personnel Director.

It is true that some aspects of manager development are intangible. It is equally true that the really effective development plans are regarded as economic activities of the business. When their costs are challenged they can be justified in positive, identifiable improvements in jobs and managers. Where the wish to evaluate critically is absent, management development becomes a flabby complacent routine.

B. THE CHIEF EXECUTIVE'S VIEW.

We recently made a study (18) of the attitude of Chief Executives to the problem of developing their managers. The growth in their interest in this subject was due to six main pressures:

First, the increased complexity of a manager's job in the face of an accelerating rate of technological change, the larger size of business and the introduction of new tools such as the computer caused concern. Many managers are inadequate because the job has outgrown them. 'Management obsolescence' is a genuine issue, not a conference joke. It is recognized that unless much more attention is given at the planning stage to developing people's knowledge and skills, important new projects and techniques will be stultified.

Second, the failure to produce enough men of general management outlook. The shortage of general managers has been particularly evident when large companies have decentralized their operations and have had to face complex new problems of co-ordination and control. The need to ensure that specialists improve their performance and have an opportunity to accept wider responsibilities is obvious. Over-specialization for too long has become common and Chief Executives believe that there is now no alternative to selecting a group of able men, relatively young, and grooming them deliberately for general management.

Third, succession problems are commonplace in every type of business. Some Chief Executives admitted that they were interested in management development because they had lost key executives and found no one remotely eligible to replace them from within the business. The ratio of managers to work force is much higher than it used to be and calls for a greater number of managers. Since the problem is universal, the main solution is recognized as 'developing our own men' rather than constantly trying to buy in talent.

Fourth, there are doubts whether the money invested so far in management development, company training centres and so on has been really well spent. 'I'm sure we have achieved something. I'm equally sure our past efforts have not been wholly successful … but I'm continuing them as an insurance policy until something better emerges' was one comment. This is in striking contrast to the enthusiasm and confidence of the Chief Executives who have introduced an Improving Management Performance approach and discovered the lasting benefits.

Fifth, there was frank admission that companies had grown complacent in the post war sellers' market. Managers brought up in this easy going atmosphere were concerned with security, not risk taking and innovation. 'One reason why I've decentralized my operating units is to put back into people a sense of responsibility for profit and loss. How else will we create vitality and growth?' said the Managing Director of one engineering group. There is also the problem of what to do with a manager who, after many chances, cannot or will not match up to the job standard. "Let's face it, most of us lack the moral courage to deal with this as we should, especially when it is a man who has given his life to the business" was one view. Probably it represents a general truth, even though other Chief Executives were quick to point out that firmness in these cases was in the interest not only of the business but also of the man himself. Another view was "My philosophy is to set a time limit and a measurable target for minimum performance and then do everything I can to help the man succeed. If he doesn't, I remove him from his post although I then treat him with generous consideration."

Sixth, those companies with overseas subsidiaries commented on the pressures of nationalism. Long term plans to hand over to nationals were having to be compressed into much shorter periods. It was felt that more attention would have to be given to analysing the present managerial knowledge and skills in detail, thus making it possible for more concentrated instruction to be given.

Compared with a similar study made some years ago, there was a widespread and fundamental change in attitude. Chief Executives today recognize more than ever before that their managers are a precious capital resource which requires the same systematic attention as financial and physical resources.

Asked what they wanted from a management development programme, Chief Executives said:

1. To have an effective method of defining results expected from managers.

2. To get managers continuously to improve their performance.

3. To secure and hold recruits of suitable calibre.

4. To provide first class training, for tomorrow's job as well as today's, at lower cost.

5. To have a reliable means of judging the performance of managers.
6. To have a flexible succession plan for staffing the business in the future.
7. To motivate managers and reward them fairly in relation to the results achieved.
8. To improve the flow of communications up, down and across the business.

C. THE MANAGER'S NEEDS.

There is a preoccupation with the Chief Executive's viewpoint and the methods which he can use to improve his managers. It is illuminating to see these methods in relation to the manager's needs. A typical manager, when asked 'What do you want from me, your boss, in order to perform your job better' would have five needs:

The manager's needs	Methods available to help the manager
'Tell me what you expect from me'	Clarifying *Unit Objectives* and priorities for Improvement *Key Results Analysis* with Performance Standards *Job Improvement Plans*
'Give me an opportunity to perform'	*Organization Planning*
'Let me know how I'm getting on'	*Control Information* *Performance Review*
'Give me guidance where I need it'	*Management Development Methods:* – Potential Review
'Reward me according to my contribution'	– Training – Salary structure – Succession Plans

TYPICAL LAUNCHING SEQUENCE

EXHIBIT 8

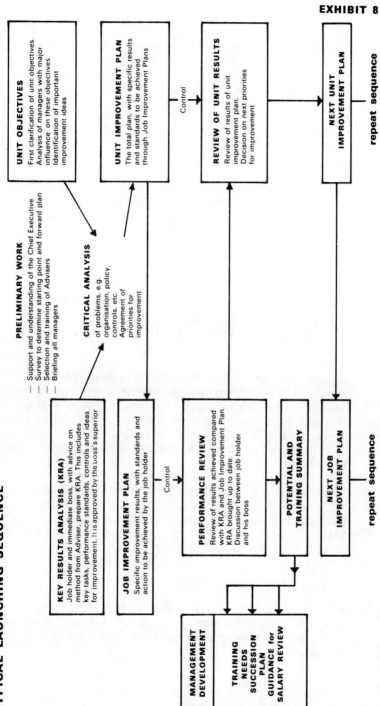

PRELIMINARY WORK
— Support and understanding of the Chief Executive
— Survey to determine starting point and forward plan
— Selection and training of Advisers
— Briefing all managers

UNIT OBJECTIVES
First clarification of unit objectives. Analysis of managers with major influence on these objectives Identification of important improvement ideas

CRITICAL ANALYSIS
of problems, e.g. organisation, policy, controls, etc. Agreement of priorities for improvement

UNIT IMPROVEMENT PLAN
The total plan, with specific results and standards to be achieved through Job Improvement Plans

Control

REVIEW OF UNIT RESULTS
Review of results of unit improvement plan. Decision on next priorities for improvement

NEXT UNIT IMPROVEMENT PLAN

repeat sequence

KEY RESULTS ANALYSIS (KRA)
Job holder and immediate boss, with advice on method from Adviser, prepare KRA. This includes key tasks, performance standards, controls and ideas for improvement. It is approved by the boss's superior

JOB IMPROVEMENT PLAN
Specific improvement results, with standards and action to be achieved by the job holder

Control

PERFORMANCE REVIEW
Review of results achieved compared with KRA and Job Improvement Plan. KRA brought up to date. Discussion between job holder and his boss

POTENTIAL AND TRAINING SUMMARY

NEXT JOB IMPROVEMENT PLAN

repeat sequence

MANAGEMENT DEVELOPMENT

TRAINING NEEDS
SUCCESSION PLAN
GUIDANCE for SALARY REVIEW

This simple analysis stresses the inter-relationship of needs, and therefore of supporting methods and techniques. To train a manager without a clear grasp of the skills and knowledge he requires to secure results can be frustrating. The influence of a good salary structure on motivation can be slight if the manager is bewildered about the nature of his responsibilities. Control information devised by staff specialists may prove to be irrelevant to the manager's need to know specifically if he is meeting performance standards.

Thus, success must come from the continuous satisfaction of all the manager's needs and not from spasmodically introducing isolated techniques. This integration is a vital contribution of Improving Management Performance.

III. A TYPICAL SEQUENCE FOR INTRODUC- ING AN IMPROVING MANAGEMENT PERFORMANCE PLAN

In a later section of this book, various strategies and difficulties in launching a total "Improving Business Results" programme are discussed and great emphasis is placed on the need for a thorough preliminary study. Many practical difficulties arise through failure to judge accurately the best starting point, the sophistication of techniques required, the sequence of work and so on.

However, having stressed that there is no "package deal" or "one best way", it will be convenient to describe the main features of a typical sequence for launching an Improving Management Performance plan. This sequence is illustrated in Exhibit 8 and can be summarised thus:

A. PRELIMINARY WORK.

Before the programme can be launched successfully it is necessary to gain the support of the Chief Executive of the unit, to make a forward plan, to train Advisers and to brief the managers.

58

B. CLARIFY UNIT OBJECTIVES.

The present unit objectives are clarified, and examined critically to identify the scope for improvement.

C. KEY RESULTS ANALYSIS.

Shortly afterwards, or simultaneously, the Key Results required from each manager are analysed, together with the performance standards and controls associated with them. Each manager makes his own Analysis with the help of an Adviser and the Analysis is agreed by the manager's boss and *his* superior. The scope for improvement in each job is considered.

D. CRITICAL ANALYSIS.

Top management makes a critical analysis of the evidence collected during the clarification of unit objectives and the Key Results Analysis work. They determine the priorities for improvement.

E. IMPROVEMENT PLANS FOR THE UNIT AND EACH JOB.

Top management's priorities are expressed formally in a Unit Improvement Plan for a given period and this in turn is broken down into specific responsibilities for each manager to improve his job.

F. OPPORTUNITY TO PERFORM.

The managers in an agreed time period then work to achieve their Key Results and also to secure the benefits defined in the Job Improvement Plan. Control and informal review of progress is necessary.

G. PERFORMANCE REVIEW.
The results achieved by each Manager are then systematically reviewed and discussed with him. The overall results for the Unit are summarised.

H. MANAGEMENT DEVELOPMENT.

The by-products of the Review include the assessment of potential, the identification of training needs for the managers and the establishment of a Succession Plan. The evidence is also of great value in making the salary review.

5

I. CONTINUITY.

A revised set of Unit and Job Improvement Plans is then prepared and the cycle starts again.

Each of these main stages will now be considered in more detail.

A. PRELIMINARY WORK.

There are four aspects to the preliminary work.

1. The understanding and involvement of the Chief Executive of the unit selected for pilot work must be deepened.

2. Company Advisers must be selected and trained to a high professional standard in the various techniques. The Adviser's role needs further explanation. In launching the programme there must be at least one man in the company who has the time and the expertise to counsel managers in best methods. It is not a permanent appointment and the Adviser ceases to exist in a formal sense when the difficult introductory phase ends. Indeed, it would be a definition of his failure to get the system built naturally into the management pattern if his presence was still required. The choice—and training—of this man is a most important factor in achieving success. A good first rule is "if he can be spared from his present job he isn't suitable..." and executive management experience, maturity, intelligence and open mindedness are all desirable. It is not surprising that many companies assign men of high potential to this work, recognising its broadening and demanding character. In a larger group it is common to set up Project Teams and it is helpful in these cases to have men from varied backgrounds and disciplines.

An Adviser is a source of professional advice on the whole programme. He develops suitable techniques and methods with managers; counsels each individual manager in the Key Results Analysis preparation; is present at first Reviews; helps to analyse training plans. He is an "educator" and "catalyst", *not* a man who states what the standards should be, nor what the priorities are and how the problems should be solved. That is management's task.

60

3. A plan, with time schedule and work load must be prepared. This will be a refinement of the general plan outlined during the original survey of the situation.

4. A thorough briefing of middle and lower management with an opportunity for discussion and questions must be arranged.

B. CLARIFY UNIT OBJECTIVES.

The more specific the objectives of the unit concerned—say a factory, a laboratory, a sales division, an office—the easier it is to link them directly with the objectives of the individual manager. When a company has subjected itself to a rigorous and self critical analysis and set itself objectives it is possible to move forward quickly and confidently at unit level. However, there are businesses where top management is satisfied with the clarity of company and unit objectives although in fact they are woolly and generalised. It might be necessary to start by defining Unit Objectives in order to demonstrate the *need* to review higher level goals.

Commonly, the situation lies between these extremes of virtue and vice and some objectives do exist although they are mixed in quality and perhaps narrow in range. Top management is receptive to clarifying them. In this case three steps can be taken:

1. List Primary Results Areas.

The Chief Executive and his senior team set down the framework of headings in which results are vital. They are asking themselves "In what main areas must we be able to perform well to succeed?" For example, a building company produced a first list like this:

a. The ability to estimate accurately and tender competitively and subsequently the ability to negotiate variations etc. in terms which are financially favourable.

b. The ability to win a planned, stable and expanding share of the type of contracts we know we are good at.

61

c. The ability to increase the range and scale of work we are good at.

d. The ability to accumulate or attract adequate capital into the business to finance operations.

e. The ability to plan and control operations from the pre-tender stage through to completion so that our reputation for completion on time is maintained.

f. The ability to recruit, train and retain a loyal and effective management and supervisory team and to utilise them in an effective manner.

g. The ability to establish and sustain a high level of work output per direct operator.

h. The ability to achieve a high rate of return on investments in plant and machinery.

i. The ability to buy materials at competitive prices and schedule them in a manner which minimises production delays etc.

j. The ability to control quality and minimise client claims for bad workmanship.

k. The ability to inculcate a disciplined attitude to site safety.

l. The ability to negotiate advantageous associations with other firms (i.e. consortia) and find profitable opportunities to diversify or expand the Company's activities,

or in more conventional terms:

a. PROFITABILITY.

b. LEVEL OF ACTIVITY or TURNOVER.

c. SIZE OF CONTRACTS.

d. AVAILABILITY OF WORKING CAPITAL.

e. ACHIEVEMENT OF CONTRACT PROGRAMMES.

f. MANAGER PERFORMANCE.

g. LABOUR PERFORMANCE or PRODUCTIVITY.

h. PLANT UTILISATION.

i. MATERIAL UTILISATION & COST

j. ACHIEVEMENT OF ACCEPTABLE QUALITY.

k. SITE SAFETY.

l. DIVERSIFICATION OF ACTIVITIES.

Then, against each heading they considered present specific objectives, important problems and opportunities.

2. Identify Secondary Results Areas.

For each Primary Result Area a number of Secondary Results can be identified. For example, a Primary Result area for the maintenance department of a chemical works was

SERVICE i.e. providing a maintenance service which contributes to good plant results.

The Secondary Results were identified as:

— proportion of critical equipment out of commission;
— proportion of downtime;
— number of overdue jobs;
— time required for shutdowns.

This more detailed breakdown is usually unnecessary for all the Primary Results areas since it is better to select those where problems or opportunities of a significant kind have been identified.

3. Construct a Results Influence Chart.

Brief discussion with each of the managers will quickly indicate on which Results areas they have a major influence and what problems they are meeting. A simple chart can then be prepared on the basis:

Result Area / Manager	Production Manager	Senior Foreman Shop 1	Sales Manager
SERVICE			
1. Equipment out of commission	✓	✗	✗
2. Down time	✓	✓	✗
3. Overdue jobs	✓	✓	✗

EXHIBIT 9

I. MAIN PURPOSE OF JOB.
(State the main contribution of the job to the efficient working of the Company.)
To ensure that the Company's products are manufactured to the technical specifications a cost to meet Sales Departments delivery requirements.

II. POSITION IN ORGANISATION.
  (a) Directly responsible to:
      Managing Director
  (b) Subordinates directly supervised:
      Machine Shop Superintendent   Chief Planning Engineer
      Tool Room Foreman   Progress Manager
      Heat Treatment Foreman   Production Control Manager
      Foundry Foreman   Works Engineer

IV. KEY TASKS.

Description of key task	Level of performance
1. *Delivery*. To ensure that manufacturing orders are delivered on time.	When 90% of all orders placed on the delivered within the standard cycle ti When no order is late by more than half cycle time. When the standard cycle times do those specified.
2. *Output*. To ensure that the Works achieves a satisfactory level of output.	When output reaches not less than budgeted output.
3. *Use of Resources*. To ensure that the most effective use is made of available resources.	*Labour:* When average waiting time never ex in any month. When ratio of direct to indirect labo exceed 4.0. When labour turnover, including staf exceed 15% pa. When pay performance is 95%. *Machines:* Average machine utilisation never falls No machine is utilised for less than 35% *Floor Space:* When not less than 90% factory floor area is utilised for produc *Stocks:* When the money utilised in stocks never exceeds the specified fi
4. *Costs*. To ensure that manufacturing costs are kept to a minimum consistent with achieving other objectives.	When fixed overhead expenses never Budget. When variable overhead expenses ne the Budget. When no variance on any item of e exceeds the standard by more than 5%
5. *Quality*. To ensure that the work reaches the required quality levels.	When the cost of scrap never exceeds month. When not more than 3% of all comp rejected. When excessively stringent require always taken up with the designer.

V. PERSONAL ACTIVITIES.
(List these activities actually performed by you, and not delegated. Items included here wil the Key Tasks.)
Appointment of supervisors.
Disciplinary action on senior staff.
Performance reviews of subordinates, etc., etc.

PART OF THE KEY RESULTS ANALYSIS
FOR A PRODUCTION MANAGER ([19])

. OF THE JOB.
te your total responsibilities in terms of men, materials and facilities.)

nel	No.	Wages £000's	Materials	Average stock values:
	205	188		£
t	51	35	Raw materials	9,000
	29	23	Work in Progress	28,000
		——	Consumable Stores	8,000
		£246	Finished Parts	48,000
				93,000

Plant
Replacement cost, total: £700,000

used for measuring performance	Suggestions or comments
urns of delivery performance.	This control information is not available at present, and is to be instituted immediately.
urns of delivery performance.	
programme, and weekly returns of erformance.	Capacity of the machine shop by types needs to be determined.
d monthly output statistics.	
m wages office.	
heck on personnel records.	
heck on personnel records.	
m Wages Office.	
information available at present. information available at present. eck on floor area by Works Engineers.	This information will be produced by adopting suggestions mentioned in I above.
ccounts.	These figures are based on experience; suggest a project be carried out to determine optimum figures.
ccounts.	
ccounts.	
ccounts.	
ccounts.	
port from Inspection Dept.	
ction.	

S OF AUTHORITY.
 in this section will normally concern some or all of the following—physical resources, personnel,
 al commitments.)
 uthorise overhauls and capital expenditure up to £500.
 gage staff within budget.
 der and stock materials, etc.

EXHIBIT 10

EXTRACT FROM KEY RESULTS [20]
ANALYSIS OF A
RESEARCH MANAGER

Description of Key Tasks	Level of Performance	Controls used to measure	Suggestions
(1) New Products (offensive research)			
1.1 To collect all ideas for new products from all possible sources. To segregate the good from the bad and to align the good with company objectives.	No idea eliminated at this stage and later found to be providing profitable business for a competitor (unless idea was rejected through non-alignment with objectives—see 1.2 below).	Register of all ideas and decisions. List of competitors' new products.	
1.2 To recognise competitors' technological strategy and to advise M.D. when objectives should be modified.	Company's marketing and operating programmes never require "crash" changes due to failure to recognise competitors' technological strategy.	No record needed. Any such occurrence will be recognised by all.	Our methods of collecting news of competitors' technological strategy need improving. (See improvement plan for first half of 1966.)
1.3 To submit to New Product Committee recommendations for undertaking R and D or seeking licences for new products or improved quality of existing products. Cases to be fully documented with estimated share of market, profitability, etc.	No case ever to be referred back for more information. New Product Committee to accept at least 80% of the recommendations as feasible for eventual implementation.	Record of cases submitted, referred back, accepted and rejected (maintained by secretary of committee). Current selection criterion is that present value of future gross trading profits shall be greater than twice present value of anticipated investment.	Close liaison with Marketing must be maintained. M.D. to discuss with Marketing Manager the need to second a full-time marketing officer to R and D. Chairman of new products committee should watch the "success ratio."
1.4 To submit to New Product	No project to be carried on more than	Cost returns	

...ed processes and to segregate the good from the bad.	...that process productivity can be increased by 4% p.a.		increased from 34% to 38%. Action by M.D. to discuss with C.A.
2.2 To monitor changes in quality of competitive products.	Marketing department warned when significant changes occur that could affect share of market.	Quality lab. test reports.	
(3) Laboratory Management			
3.1 To direct, supervise and assist all Section Leaders and to advise Research Scientists during their work.	75% of all projects and investigations to be completed satisfactorily within the time and cost originally budgeted. The balance of 25% to be completed within the original estimate plus one supplementary estimate of extra time and cost.	Project cost sheets. "Satisfactory" shall mean that the Executive Committee accept 90% or more of the recommendations for future action put up by A.L. Brown.	We must train our Research Scientists to write better reports and to develop a better commercial sense. (See improvement plan for first half of 1966.)
3.2 To arrange for training at all levels by all means.	Planned growth rate is 8% p.a. and 75% of the section leaders and upwards posts are to be filled from within.	Personnel records.	
3.3 To create and maintain good morale.	Staff turnover to be kept below 15% (males) and 25% (females).	Personnel department turn-over return.	
(4) State of the Art To build up and maintain the company's reputation as one of the four leaders in the technology of the business.	At least six papers to be published per annum in leading technical journals.	Librarian's list. Joint papers with Research Association will count. Invitations to address major conferences and seminars will also count.	Open up more channels of communication with Universities and "CATs". Action by M.D. and Research Manager jointly.
(5) Patent Strategy To ensure that all patentable ideas are protected.	No occurrence of curtailed sales or litigation or serious change in R and D programme due to failure to protect at the right time.	Occurrences will be known.	

C. KEY RESULTS ANALYSIS.

Whilst unit objectives are being clarified, Key Results Analyses are often prepared for managers within the unit. Some flexibility in approach is essential, however. If the work on unit objectives reveals organisational weaknesses, for example, it may be wasteful to do a *thorough* job of analysis on individual jobs when it is known that they will be changed. In such a case a much simpler analysis would be adequate. For convenience at this stage we will assume that it is appropriate to make a full Analysis. Exhibits 9 and 10 show extracts from Key Results Analysis forms.

Clearly these Analyses are vastly different from traditional lists of "duties and responsibilities" which are usually generalised and lengthy, rather than specific, and may confuse the manager's activities with the end result of these activities. To say of a Production Manager that he is responsible for "reviewing the company's manufacturing operations, in order to ensure a high level of effectiveness" is to say virtually nothing. Moreover, such statements invariably do not differentiate the vital profit influencing element from the trivial, and may crystallize the present without providing impetus for future improvement. A Key Result Analysis, by definition, does not attempt to list *all* a manager's tasks.

1. *Don't managers already know what is expected of them?*

There is a general belief that managers know what is expected of them even though it may not be written down. 'After all' said one General Manager of his Superintendent, 'He's been doing the job for eight years. If he doesn't know what is expected of him by now, what have I been paying him for?'

In practice many managers *are* unclear about the results they must achieve and these doubts are a potent cause of personal insecurity and conservatism.

Our experience is supported by research studies. In a survey (21) of 500 members, the British Institution of Works Managers

68

asked each to pick from a questionnaire of 52 items the most serious factors restricting productivity in his company. "Frustration at all levels due to lack of clearly defined spheres of delegated responsibilities" was high on the list. At a lower management level, a British Department of Scientific and Industrial Research study (22) of the 'Supervisor and his job', covering five companies in a cross section of industries concluded "The study has revealed differences in the functions of supervisors, not only between individual firms but also between individuals and jobs in the same firm. These variations are so great and the factors influencing them so complex, that managers cannot assume they have an intimate knowledge of these functions, either on a basis of prediction from experience or even by a consideration of existing job specifications which may bear little relation to the facts. There is no substitute for the direct observation of each supervisory job." When Drs. N. F. Maier and L. R. Hoffman of the University of Michigan conducted detailed interviews with 222 managerial 'pairs', as part of a study (23) of differences in job perception between boss and subordinate, only 8.1 per cent showed almost complete agreement. In relation to obstacles in the way of effective subordinate performance there was almost complete disagreement on obstacles in 38.6 per cent of the 'pairs'.

In an Engineering Company (24) it is reported that "... the stated, most important objective in the eyes of top management was an improvement in the poor delivery situation. Yet during a survey of individual managers' priorities, only 1 out of 86 in the Production Department saw this as his responsibility and no regular information on deliveries was available to many of them."

2. Practical points in completing the Analysis.

As the Exhibits illustrate, there are four columns—Key Tasks, Performance Standards, Controls and Suggestions.

Key Tasks.

In this column are listed the small number of tasks which will have a major impact on success. If searching work has been done in identifying Unit Objectives it is obviously much easier

to start the manager off with a framework of his key tasks. In any case, we should ask for *this* job, with Drucker: (25)
'in what areas would excellence really have an extraordinary impact on the economic results of our business, to the point where it might transform the economic performance of the entire business?' 'In what areas would poor performance threaten to damage economic performance, greatly or at least significantly?'

Such statements of Key Tasks as

— "to achieve the budgeted level of sales"
— "to control scrap level"
— "to ensure that factory capacity is fully utilised"

are good because performance standards will develop naturally from them.

When the Key Tasks are listed and agreed, then each one is taken in turn and considered in terms of Performance Standards, Controls, Suggestions for Improvement.

Performance Standards.

A performance standard is 'a statement of the conditions which exist when the required result is being satisfactorily achieved'. It is not a statement of the ideal standard in ideal circumstances nor the minimum acceptable standard. It must be realistic yet challenging. Performance standards are of two main categories:

Measured or Quantitative, i.e., those standards which can be expressed in terms such as:

— goods produced per month
— cost levels
— market penetration per product
— per cent delay time
— ratios of return on investment
— scrap levels
— turnover
— inventory level.

Wherever possible, quantitative standards are sought and

often these can be developed where at first sight only subjective opinions appear to be available.

Judged or Qualitative, i.e., those standards which although not directly measurable in quantitative terms can be verified by judgment and observation. For example:
'Key Results Analysis and Improvement Plans issued to all immediate subordinates and revised annually.'

A standard must define an end result, not an action so that

'To visit my branch'

is unsatisfactory since it does not indicate the expected result from the visit.

In relation to Measured and Judged Standards it may help to look for standards which relate to

— QUANTITY (How much?)
— QUALITY (How well?)
— TIME (By what time?)
— COST (At what cost?)

Poor standards can often be detected by looking for the use of such words as:

'adequate'

'approximately'

'few'

'as soon as possible'

'reasonable'

'minimum'

'desirable'

Many performance standards already exist in a business through budgets, allocations, technical specifications and so on; but they are rarely seen in an integrated management pattern, linked with key results and controls.

Clearly performance standards relate to the job, since they link back to unit and company objectives, and not to the job holder. Moreover, key results and performance standards must be

71

consistent within a company although parochialism can be expected in the first drafts. For example, a production unit which sets a high quality standard without reference to the market standard as required by the customer and identified by the sales department, may be pursuing an apparently worthy aim which is not in the wider company interest.

It is difficult to establish good standards for advisory and staff jobs and Advisers should be thoroughly trained in this area or poor quality work will emerge. To illustrate this, take the example of a Works Accountant who had as one of his key tasks:

"To provide a management control data and cost data service to line management."

The Performance Standards defined by the Accountant, working on his own, were:

"a. When control statements are being issued to line managers as soon as possible after the period to which they refer (a TIME standard).

b. When an adequate amount of control information is being supplied to all appropriate managers (a HOW MUCH standard).

c. When the cost information being provided is being used and is having a desirable effect on costs (a HOW WELL standard).

d. When the cost of producing the control information is at a minimum (an AT WHAT COST standard)."

Although this may look impressive it really did little to clarify the situation. A skilled Adviser helped the Works Accountant to go deeper in his analyses:

"a. Weekly control statements are issued not later than two weeks after the period to which they refer.

b. Monthly control statements are issued not later than two weeks after the period to which they refer (both TIME standards).

c. Control information is being supplied to line managers covering all the measurable standards of performance referred to in their Key Results Analyses (a HOW MUCH standard).

d. Control statements clearly indicate reasons and responsibilities for variances (a HOW WELL standard).

e. Managers are controlling expenditure within 5% of budget (a HOW WELL standard).

f. The clerical and stationery cost of producing the required periodic control information does not exceed £8,000. per year (a possible AT WHAT COST standard)."

This example illustrates another important facet of setting performance standards. The Accountant and his Adviser had to decide whether the standards should refer to conditions *as they are now* or *as they could be* or *as they should be*. Taking the example of standard b. above, which refers to the time lag in issuing monthly statements, the actual situation was that they were then being issued up to three weeks after the reference period. In the course of setting the standard it was agreed that a two week lag was feasible but that the ultimate aim must be to so change the methods that the delay was only four days. Under these circumstances, the performance standard agreed is two weeks i.e. this is what can reasonably be expected without any major change in organisation or procedure. The possibility of achieving a four day standard would go into the "Suggestions" column. Subsequently the action necessary to achieve it could go into the Accountant's own Job Improvement Plan. If many individuals were involved or, say, the computer's help was required the action might form part of the total Unit Improvement Plan.

Controls.

In relation to each established standard the manager now answers the question 'How will I know whether I'm securing agreed results?' After all, without this feedback even a manager with clear objectives can steadily be drifting off course without knowing it.

Controls will usually be a specific document where the standard is quantitative—"labour cost control statement, issued weekly", "Budget variance analysis, available monthly" and so on. It is rarely desirable to have more than one control for each standard.

Sometimes the only control is qualitative i.e. what the manager's boss judges to be on standard and in these cases it may be useful to state on what he will base his judgment.

73

For some standards there may be no control at all. This is a clear signal that a control must be established or that the standard is not as important as was first thought. The manager may find that he has a mass of control information not related to standards and he must then challenge whether it should continue to be issued.

More comments on control information will be made later in this book.

Suggestions.

The manager, counselled and stimulated by the Adviser, will then look critically at the first three columns of the Analysis. A Key Result Analysis does not merely define more clearly the present situation but it challenges every aspect of it. In the 'Suggestions' column a manager records his ideas for improvement. The number and quality of suggestions is a useful indicator to the thoroughness of the Key Results Analysis. For example, (26)

In the manufacturing part of one engineering company, involving 47 managers at various levels down to foreman, 240 suggestions and comments were made, referring to 145 different ideas. As might be expected, these were of varying value and importance. However, those occurring most frequently were, by definition, felt to be genuine needs by a majority of managers. The 10 most frequently made suggestions were:

SUGGESTIONS	No. of Originators		Status of Originators			
	Total	per cent	Mgr.	Dep. Mgr.	Sptdt.	Foreman
1. Cost information should be issued more promptly and should be clearer . .	18	38	2	3	5	8
2. Tool delivery service should be improved . .	11	23	1	—	4	6

SUGGESTIONS	No. of Originators		Status of Originators			
	Total	per cent	Mgr.	Dep. Mgr.	Sptdt.	Foreman
3. Materials handling should be improved, particularly to avoid double handling, and to improve reliability of trucks . . .	11	23	—	—	4	7
4. Planned maintenance for production and process plant	10	21	1	1	3	5
5. Tool usage should be analysed and reduced . .	9	19	—	—	3	6
6. Breakdown maintenance should be improved and better service given to reduce waiting time . . .	8	17	1	—	2	5
7. Work in progress should be reduced	6	13	1	1	1	3
8. Incentive scheme for indirect labour should be revised	6	13	—	2	2	2
9. Raw material quality should be improved by better inspection	5	11	1	—	1	3
10. Obsolete tool stock should be removed . . .	4	9	1	—	1	2

3. Who is directly involved?

Each manager prepares his own Key Result Analysis, with the Adviser to guide him on method—the content of the first draft is entirely the manager's final responsibility. This draft is then reviewed, discussed and amended in a session between the manager, his boss and the Adviser. Finally the boss's superior also approves the final statement. In this way there is:

— the fullest opportunity for three levels of management to **make a** constructive contribution;

6

— less danger of low or unrealistic standards being developed, or prejudice creeping in;

— a wider view taken of individual and departmental objectives to confirm that they are directed to company goals.

Should a manager disagree with his boss, the boss must of course retain the right to have his way. In practice this occurs infrequently. Where the right climate of opinion has been created both men are sincerely searching for the truth and accept the 'Law of the situation'. Where a number of managers are doing *exactly* the same job, usually a shift operation, the discussion may take place between all job holders and their boss, as a group discussion.

4. Isn't this bureaucratic?

The first reaction of some people to Key Results Analysis is that it is over-elaborate; or it will take too much time; or it will limit personal initiative. Certainly, the first completion of a Key Results Analysis will take several hours, but thereafter it only needs to be brought up to date regularly or when the job itself changes fundamentally. If there is already clear understanding between manager and boss then the Analysis will take an hour! The fact that this is a rare event confirms our experience that this searching analysis illuminates unexpected areas of uncertainty and misunderstanding. In any case, the common attitude: "We are far too busy doing jobs which we have never had time to spell out in specific terms" must lead to dissipated effort. Agreeing with a man what results he is expected to achieve is a fundamental business and human need, not a luxury or "optional extra". Because of this it must be done thoroughly and with patience, not rushed through in order to produce another form. How many traditional "duties and responsibilities" are read, filed and forgotten because they *are* superficial?

Does the clarity of a Key Results Analysis diminish initiative? The opposite is true since a manager can act more confidently and purposefully if his goals and authority are clear. His freedom is still great. The Key Results Analysis probably covers only the 15% of his total tasks which are vital and leaves him great discretion in the others. In all tasks the concern is with *results,* leaving the manager to achieve them in his own style. This is a way to give a manager maximum freedom "within the Law", the Law being the framework of unit objectives and policy. Complete freedom brings anarchy in an organisation and in any case as Wilfred Brown points out (27) 'If every time a manager faces a problem his first thought is "Is it my responsibility to deal with this or not?", then a state of uncertainty develops which *impedes* initiative.'

D. CRITICAL ANALYSIS.

At this stage of launching a programme of Improving Management Performance it is timely to examine critically the data which has been collected, in order to determine the most profitable areas for improvement.

The evidence available includes:

— present unit objectives and ideas on problems and constraints and opportunities;

— an indication through the Results Influence chart of the way in which the work to be done is divided organisationally;

— summaries of ideas and suggestions from Key Results Analyses.

The evidence is studied by top management, with support from the Adviser and perhaps other specialists whose opinion is thought to be useful. It is possible to draw up a tentative first list of problems and opportunities in simple statements such as:

"Key Results Analyses show that there is serious overlap between our four levels of factory supervision. It appears that certainly three and possibly only two levels will be required in future."

"District Sales Managers do not know the profit margins on the main product lines and there are cases where they have focussed their effort and increased turnover on lines where we lose money, because of their lack of knowledge."

"The salary structure and levels for middle management in our subsidiary companies vary greatly. This is proving to be a major difficulty in transferring key men between the companies."

"We have an expensive legal department of our own. The Key Results Analysis shows that 80% of the work they do is simple conveyancing which could be done equally well and much more economically by outside solicitors. Should we radically reduce the size of the department and sub-contract this routine work?"

"We have very tight control over labour costs but primitive control over material costs. This is unsound when material $= 56\%$ of selling price and labour only $= 9\%$. This suggests the need for better materials management and also the dangers of letting production oriented workstudy men devise management controls."

Quite often the list includes important and complicated problems which are already well known to management but for which no solution has been found. The attitude to these problems is often one of resigned acceptance—"We just have to live with it" and mutual recrimination—"How can production do a better job when sales behave as they do?" It often pays to take this type of important problem and get a small team of four or five managers who have a direct influence on it to explore possibilities more fully, with the Adviser acting as catalyst again. This has the advantages of:

— creating a genuine sense of common interest in starting to solve together difficulties believed to be intractable

— multi-function stimulus and contribution can get useful "immediate" action under way as well as setting out the objectives which need more thorough consideration;

— the results of their discussion can be expressed in terms of:
Where does the opportunity for improvement lie?
What do we want to achieve?
What are the obstacles in our way?
What can we do—now and in the next year?

The Adviser should, in his initial training, become expert in the group methods which have been developed to make these sessions really fruitful.

EXHIBIT 11

CRITICAL ANALYSIS

THE PROBLEM

Inadequate planned maintenance in the factory is responsible for excessive downtime on the key stripping machines.

THE OBJECTIVE

To have worked out and applied a system of planned maintenance for the stripping machines so that downtime is no greater than 2%.

ACTION

	Job Improvement Plan reference for manager responsible for action	
1. A maintenance scheme to have been worked out for two selected machines by November 1966.	Works Engineer Production Manager	JIP 4 JIP 1
2. A trial of six months to be carried out and results evaluated in financial and production terms and compared with the highest standards achieved elsewhere in the world to the knowledge of the machinery manufacturer.	Works Engineer Production Manager	JIP 5 JIP 2
3. Fitters and electricians to be trained in faults analysis and trouble shooting methods after detailed study of their work through skills analysis methods. Trial machine fitters and electricians to be trained by November 1966 and the remainder by April 1967.	Training Officer Fitter Foreman Electrician Foreman	JIP 2 JIP 3 (b) JIP 5

EXAMPLE OF A CRITICAL ANALYSIS STUDY

Exhibit 11 shows the typical end product of such a session in which a series of clear actions are to be taken as part of a Unit Improvement Plan to improve a worrying and long established problem.

E. IMPROVEMENT PLANS FOR THE UNIT AND EACH JOB.

From the final summary top management has to make its choice of priorities for improvement and consider the resources which will be required. Whilst recognising the need to set a challenge, nothing can be more destructive of morale than to have a series of attractive Improvement Plans which are unrealistic. It brings the whole programme into disrespect and creates the attitude of mind that "these improvement plans are really an optional extra. Very nice if you can achieve them but understandable if you don't."

Top management will then make a UNIT IMPROVEMENT PLAN setting out specifically the objectives for improvement, the performance standards and time scale. This PLAN is reviewed critically and approved by the higher level manager with overall responsibility for the unit. This is a further check that the unit is working in line with wider company priorities, and not initiating worthwhile local improvements which conflict with company or other unit plans. For example, each of two subsidiary companies made the suggestion that they would like to set up a technical information library to improve research and laboratory performance. It was more economic to set up a first class library to serve them both.

The Unit Improvement Plan is then broken down into a series of results required by the various managers within the unit, and these are expressed in the form of a JOB IMPROVEMENT PLAN. The JOB IMPROVEMENT PLAN has the following characteristics:

— together with the Key Results Analysis it is the means by which every manager understands what important results he must produce in a given period;

— the Job Improvement Plan is very flexible and can readily be amended if the priorities do change. The Key Results Analysis will be relatively static unless there is a fundamental change in the nature of the job;

80

- the prime content of the Job Improvement Plan is derived from the Unit Improvement Plan;
- in addition, improvements which relate only to the individual manager's job or section are usually included also;
- the same form is often used to include items of training and development for the individual.

Once it is agreed and issued the Job Improvement Plan is vitally important. The manager is committed to achieving the results and his boss is committed to providing any agreed resources and information. If the circumstances change so that the agreed results are unlikely to be achieved the manager must refer this back to his boss. Alterations in standards should not be lightly made since the manager is responsible for finding alternative means to achieve good end results, not just abdicating when difficulties arise. Certainly, a manager who does not report to his boss that the results are unlikely to be achieved at the time genuine setbacks occur is failing in a fundamental responsibility.

Unless there is rigorous definition of improvement results, with time and performance standards and an insistence on the benefits being realised the process will be treated casually.

F. OPPORTUNITY TO PERFORM.

At this stage each manager has his Key Results Analysis and a Job Improvement Plan so that he is quite clear about what is expected of him. He then has an opportunity to perform his tasks and to get the results. The time span before a formal review is made varies according to the type of business and level of management post; at middle and lower levels three months is usually long enough. During this "opportunity to perform" period the normal management control will be exercised. The manager will seek advice on problems he cannot himself solve, whilst his boss in the normal process of discussions and meetings will be checking on progress and results.

G. PERFORMANCE REVIEW.

There is a great deal of confusion about Performance Review and its relationship with Potential Review and Salary Review.

This important subject will be considered fully in the next section, on Management Development.

At this stage of launching an Improving Management Performance programme, Performance Review is seen in two very simple ways:

1. Day to day review.

That is the normal and regular manager's job of discussing progress with his subordinates so that any correction or support can be provided.

2. Performance review.

That is the formal and disciplined check on results at pre-determined dates. For example, if the company has set up three monthly Improvement Plans for the Unit and Jobs, then a Performance Review should take place each quarter. The manager and his boss check to see if the Key Results and the Job Improvement Plans were achieved and to discuss action to decide on the *next* Improvement Plan. If they have done their day to day job properly this formal review *should* not bring any great surprises to either man. The fact that it often does is one justification for the extra discipline. Once a year they will do a rather fuller Review and think about training needs for the manager and check carefully to see the Key Results Analysis is up to date.

The boss's superior will check these Reviews also

Performance Review is a basic management tool and should not be thought about as a 'personnel procedure'.

H. MANAGEMENT DEVELOPMENT.

The management development "by-products" of the programme so far carried out will include:

1. *Potential and Training Review*
2. *Training Plans*

3. *Salary Structure and Review*

4. *Succession Plans*

Each of these aspects of management development will now be considered:

1. *Potential and Training Review: perspective.*

It will be useful to define four types of Review in order to distinguish the special characteristics of Potential and Training Review. Recent research studies underline some important basic principles and these with practical experience make it possible to suggest some guidelines for good reviews.

a. *Types of Review.* The four types of review are:

Type	Purpose	Frequency
Informal, normal Management review	This is the regular management process in which the manager and his boss assess progress through normal meetings, control data, conversations and meetings and take action to remove any obstacles.	As required maybe daily, weekly etc.
Performance Review	This is a formal Review in which the questions posed are: "We agreed on the Key Results and the Job Improvement Plan. Did we get the planned results? If not, why? What do we plan to do in our next Improvement Plan? The Review is made by the manager and his boss and fully discussed. The boss's superior will in turn check it.	This varies but a 3 monthly Performance Review is common.

Type	Purpose	Frequency
Performance Review (contd.)	At least once a year the Performance Review will include an analysis of Training Needs to do the present job better and the Key Results Analysis is critically examined and brought up to date. The Performance Review is a basic 'business' tool, concerned with checking planned results and setting new objectives.	
Potential and Training Review	Quite separately from. Performance Review it is necessary to consider a manager's potential and training needs. Against the background of his record of performance his strengths and weaknesses can be analysed: — is he placed in the most suitable job? — should he be transferred? — is he ready for promotion? — if so when and what kind of job? — are there personal factors, such as health to be taken into consideration in planning his career. It is convenient, at the same time, to summarise the manager's training needs in relation to — *present job*, as identified in the Performance Reviews;	Annually

Type	Purpose	Frequency
Potential and Training Review (contd.)	— *possible next* job as identified in the Potential Summary; — *changes in company methods, technology* etc., as identified by senior management. The Potential and Training Review is completed by the manager's boss and checked by the boss's superior. The training needs will later be discussed between manager and his boss. It may be inappropriate to discuss *all* aspects of potential. If the company employs a Personnel Manager he can play a useful role in helping the manager's boss to prepare this Review. This is in contrast with Performance Review in which the presence of the Personnel Manager is inappropriate.	
Salary Review	To decide on the change in a manager's salary and/or bonus pattern.	Annual review is common. Sometimes more frequent for junior managers.

b. *Recent research studies.*

Although Management Performance Reviews and Potential and Training Reviews—sometimes called appraisal or staff reports—are clearly important management tools, they have aroused great controversy, emotion and confusion in the last decade.

Most managers agree that the idea of systematically reviewing a subordinate's performance and discussing results with him is sound. It enables the individual to know where he stands and provides him with an opportunity to talk about his problems. Through Potential and Training Review the company is able to build up data on which to base its succession and training plans. With all these virtues it is perhaps surprising that reviews in most companies are usually imposed on line managers and arouse passive, if not open, resistance. The cynicism of line managers has, in recent years, been matched by the disillusionment felt by personnel specialists with traditional methods. Indeed, the late Douglas McGregor believed that the wrong type of review is not merely unhelpful, but positively harmful. He wrote (28):

"The conventional approach, unless handled with consummate skill and delicacy, constitutes something close to a violation of the integrity of the personality. Managers are uncomfortable when they are put into the position of playing God. The respect we hold for the inherent value of the individual leaves us distressed when we must take the responsibility for judging the personal worth of a fellow man. Yet the conventional approach to performance appraisal forces us, not only to make such judgments and to see them acted upon, but also to communicate them to those we have judged. Small wonder we resist."

Two recently published studies give us insight into the operation of, and problems arising from, management review schemes in a cross section of British and American companies.

In Great Britain, Miss Kay H. Rowe reported in 1964 (29) on a two-year research project sponsored by the Department of Scientific and Industrial Research and designed to find out how appraisals or reviews by managers of their subordinates worked in practice. 1,440 completed review forms, drawn from six companies with well-established schemes were examined and further evidence secured by interviews and questionnaires. Three main conclusions were reached:

i. *Reviewers are reluctant to review.* They do not always complete forms when required to do so; they do not always complete every section of the form as required; they do not always acknowledge authorship; the content of the entry is often evasive.

ii. *Interviewers are even more reluctant to interview.* They frequently fail to hold an interview at all and are reserved in reporting on it when they do.

iii *The follow-up is inadequate.* One reason why managers attach little importance to the forms is that the reports carry little or no weight in transfers, promotions, or training. Another is that the people to whom reports are submitted are often prepared to accept incomplete or inadequate reports without question.

As a result of this study Miss Rowe states a series of essential conditions which she considers must be met if a management review scheme is to be effective. These conditions can be summarised as follows:

— the importance of such a procedure must be made clear to all concerned. A review procedure should be instituted from the highest level as part of a management development programme, having no explicit connection with salary review;

— the calibre and status of the person given overall responsibility for administering the programme must be commensurate with the importance attached to it;

— review should be based on present performance as providing the only evidence and the only area in which a reviewer has the moral right to judge his subordinates. The reviewer should be the subordinate's immediate boss and he should also conduct the interview;

— provision must be made for participation and committal by the subordinate; in particular he must countersign the interview report and should be allowed to add his own comments if he wishes to do so;

— at every level the review procedure must be supervised by a second reviewer, i.e. the first reviewer's own boss, right up to the highest level;

— any recommendations or required action must be clearly and precisely stated;

— most vital of all, the review report must be followed up and steps taken to ensure that appropriate recommendations are implemented and the required action taken.

The American General Electric Company, recently reported (30) on a number of scientific studies made to test the effectiveness of traditional appraisal or review programmes in some of its divisions and companies. The first study brought out some interesting points, including:

— Criticism has a negative effect on achievement of goals.

— Praise has little effect one way or the other.

— Performance improves most when specific goals are established.

— Defensiveness resulting from critical appraisal produces inferior performances.

— Coaching should be a day to day, not once a year, activity.

— Mutual goal setting, not criticism, improves performance.

— Interviews designed primarily to improve a man's performance should not at the same time weigh his salary or promotion in the balance.

— Participation by the employee in the goal setting procedure helps produce favourable results.

From this and subsequent work they established a Work Planning and Review programme in which there are frequent discussions of performance without formal, written judgments or ratings being made. Separate salary discussions are held and throughout the emphasis is on mutual goal planning and problem solving. So far, encouraging results in improving job performance and increasing the amount of help managers are giving to their subordinates on the job have been identified.

c. *Guidelines for Review.*

From this research and our practical experience some guidelines can be stated:

i. *Stress the continuous nature of Performance Review.* A good manager and his boss will constantly have under review major trends in progress, serious problems and opportunities. This quick and natural feedback is essential if results are to be secured. There is an important place for the formal performance review. It is a discipline which makes sure nothing is overlooked and an occasion when a broader view of progress and the next steps can be made.

The continuous process needs stressing because many companies have an annual review which becomes a "special ceremony", at which everyone is slightly ill at ease and where people are surprised to find out that things went wrong... five months ago!

ii. *Concentrate on job performance rather than personality.* Lists of personality traits are often regarded as the important part of a Performance Review form, with job results playing a subsidiary role. This is fundamentally wrong. No one can yet define with confidence the personality profile of "the ideal manager" and in any case, how does the layman understand the precise meaning of terms such as "integrity"? or differentiate between "self-confident" and "aggressive"? Personality ratings usually lead to sterile suggestions for developing the man since it is difficult to change a mature person's personality. Managers who try to be amateur psychotherapists with their subordinates can provoke more problems than they solve. It is much more constructive to stress the *use* a man makes of his personality in achieving results. The place for comments on personality is the Potential Review form.

iii. *Encourage participation.* Participation has been an important feature of the process of agreeing the Key Results against which the Performance Review will be made. The results of review should be frankly discussed between the manager and his boss, although Miss Rowe discovered that this feature of management development was regarded with suspicion and embarrassment. This attitude stems from three main causes. First, preoccupation with personality. Most discussions about "leadership" or "acceptability" deteriorate into awkward arguments. Discussions about a previously agreed statement of expected results is constructive and less emotionally charged since as Rensis Likert puts it (31):

"People seem most willing and emotionally able to accept, and to examine in a non-defensive manner, information about themselves and their behaviour, including their inadequacies when it is in the form of *objective* evidence."

Second, overstressing the importance of an annual *discussion* when in fact Performance Reviews and re-setting short term goals should be normal routine for well organised managers.

Third, creating artificiality and self-consciousness through a mechanical approach. Whilst most managers benefit from advice on how to interview, it can create entirely the wrong atmosphere to drill them in a series of steps such as "put the man at ease; tell him his good points first" and so on. A trained Adviser sitting in on the first interviews can be very helpful, but in the end sincerity and naturalness are more important than a set of rules. After all, the manager's boss is saying in effect "You and I agreed the results and improvement objectives for this job some time ago. We've chatted about progress and handled difficulties regularly since then. Now let's stand back and have an overall look at our success, find out what went wrong and set our Improvement Plan for the next period". Note the word "we": a Performance Review is not an occasion to prove the manager guilty! After all, his failure to get results may arise from the superior's failure to provide the promised resources. A manager can and must be severely criticised, however, if he has *failed to report* earlier a change in circumstances or an unexpected problem which prevented him from performing to the agreed standard. The manager and his boss, in reviewing each Key Task might go through the thought process illustrated in Exhibit 12.

Whilst the relationship between a manager and his boss is important, the participation of the boss's superior is also necessary. He approves the manager's objectives against his broader knowledge of company priorities and discusses each review with the manager's boss. It may be more appropriate for him to discuss long-term career plans with the manager following the Potential and Training Review.

iv. *Keep Review in the hands of executive management.* Performance Reviews, and Potential and Training Reviews are not "optional extras". Every manager must help his

90

EXHIBIT 12

THE QUESTION, ANSWER & ACTION STRUCTURE OF A PERFORMANCE REVIEW MEETING

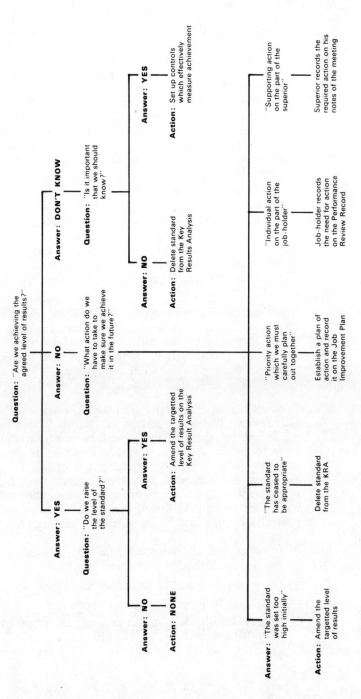

subordinates to set and achieve objectives in line with the company's plans and review results with them. Performance review is both a tool of accountability and a potent way to motivate people. It stresses a manager's role as "helper" rather than "judge" of his subordinates. Moreover, every manager must plan for the future and through Potential and Training Review he can collect sound evidence from which to build succession and training plans. Reviews which make a continuing contribution to business profitability and growth are those run by executive management.

v. *Insist on benefits.* Reviews must provoke constructive action and they should not be regarded in a negative way as tools of administration. They should be forward looking, and not just an audit of the past period. The manager should be an active agent, not a passive object to be analysed, since he must be committed to his own job results and his personal improvement.

It follows that the problems and difficulties arising from reviews must be dealt with energetically. Training programmes should be fed with sharply defined individual and group needs derived from reviews and succession plans can then be built on reliable evidence.

vi. *Distinguish sharply between Performance Review and Potential Review.* The identification of potential is certainly influenced by the manager's performance, particularly when the next possible job is similar in nature. It certainly does not follow that high performance in one job is a guarantee that a manager is certain to succeed in a higher or different position. In reviewing potential other factors which are not linked directly with performance on the present job must also be considered. They include:

— qualifications and knowledge the man posseses which are not being used in his present job;
— the man's own ambitions, drives and interests;
— the limits of his intelligence and aptitudes;
— limits of health, including for example, the temperament to withstand the strain of high office;

92

- willingness to be mobile;
- the number of years the man has to go to retirement;
- the number and scope of vacancies and the number and qualities of other candidates for the job, from inside and outside the company.

In identifying potential the contribution made by a systematic attack is to put the odds on success rather higher. In the final analysis potential is still a mystery, although we can always reassure ourselves with Jean Cocteau's aphorism "There must be such a thing as luck. How else can you account for the success of your enemies?"

vii. *The place of Salary Review.* Although a manager's worth to the company is mainly a reflection of his performance on the job and his potential, the link between Salary Review and the Performance and Potential Reviews should be indirect. Salary levels are often influenced by external factors which do not relate directly to the individual's contribution. Moreover, when performance and/or potential review and salary review recommendations are considered on one form at the same time it appears that salary considerations are dominant and much of the *development* value of the occasion is lost. Miss Rowe, for example, concludes that the appraisal procedure should have no explicit connection with salary review (32): "It would be illogical if there were wide discrepancies between appraisal and salary review but the two should be regarded as separate activities." One solution is to make salary recommendations a short time after the Potential and Training Review and also to use the evidence from the last Performance Review.

viii. *Recognise the limitations of Reviews.* Reviews can never be entirely objective. Even where good performance standards have been set the review can be poor in terms of perception of causes of failure, and insight into true training needs and so on, if the manager's boss is himself inadequate. Potential review is particularly susceptible to the "halo effect" where the boss, sometimes quite unconsciously, overestimates a man's qualities because they have common interests, or "He's always been a good chap". Conversely, prejudice and personal animosity can not be excluded.

93

First class definition of results expected and the check made by the superior of the manager's boss help, but can never entirely eliminate subjectivity.

2. *Management Training.*

The way in which training can now be provided to fit each manager's special needs is illustrated in Exhibit 13.

The weaknesses which hinder him from getting good results on his present job are identified as a by-product of Performance Review. Plans for the kind of job the manager might do in future will show that new knowledge and skills will have to be created. The *Potential* part of the 'Potential and Training Review' is the way in which these needs are determined. Finally, top management consider their forward objectives, changes in technology and methods where training is going to be important. For example, a decision to attack the French market may lead to language training for some managers. This 'company' need forms the third area of identified need.

The training summary section of the Potential and Training Review is used to summarise these needs. An examination of this summary for all managers in any group enables the forward pattern of training to be created. Group and individual plans can be established and these can form part of the Unit and Job Improvement Plans.

Finally, the normal process of Review must ensure that the planned training did take place and poses the question "Did it achieve the results we expected?"

Clearly, management training is a vast subject in its own right. In the context of an Improving Management Performance programme it may be useful to define Management Training as 'the process of developing a manager's knowledge, skills and attitudes through instruction, demonstration, practice and planned experience to meet the present and future needs of the business',

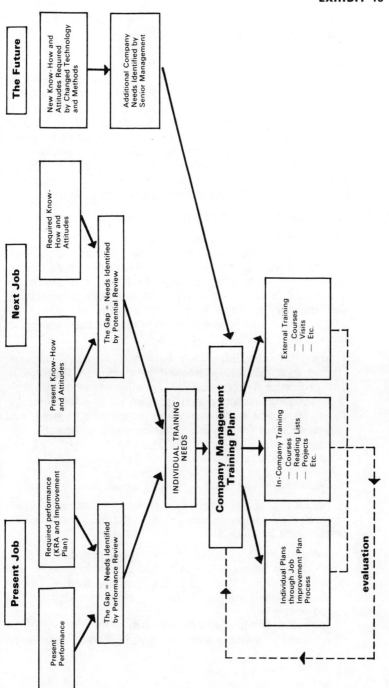

and suggest some guidelines for success:

a. *Recognise the limitations of training.*

Training *can* make an important contribution but so often too much is expected from it. A business with unsound commercial policies is not going to "train" its way out of trouble. Key managers who are still performing badly after opportunities and help to do a better job, should be removed, not sent to an advanced management course. Even the best formal instruction will fall on stony ground if the man's environment is undemanding, his responsibilities unclear or he is in a job for which his knowledge is inappropriate.

b. *Analyse training needs with great care.*

Many companies rush prematurely into training activity without being sure what the real needs are and this "shot-gun" approach is costly and ineffective. One Training Manager set up short courses on 'Human Relations' because he felt it was an 'obvious need'—later Performance Review showed that the real priorities were a better grasp of labour cost control and a refresher course on some technical aspects of the work.

Training his subordinates is a basic task for every manager, and he must be deeply involved in identifying their needs. The professional Personnel or Training Manager can help in counselling executive management on the best training and development methods; summarising common needs and presenting ideas for suitable programmes; planning the right training resources. It is *not* the Training Manager's job just to set up courses and "sell them" to line managers.

c. *Consider the individual before the group need.*

It follows that there are as many training 'problems' as there are individual managers and amongst the individual training development methods are:

i. *Job rotation.* This can provide a series of planned experiences which can help a manager to broaden in knowledge and skills. Certainly it is difficult to produce men of general management thinking if there is over specialisation for too long.
   Job rotation is fashionable and often badly used. Very little is gained by giving a manager short periods of observation

96

in a range of departments without any opportunity to become involved or to take responsibility. This is particularly true if during the period he is a supernumerary and not holding any job. There is also a danger if he does hold a job for too short a time, that he will have failed to grasp its essentials and may also disrupt the business itself. It is necessary to analyse very carefully what needs of the manager can be helped by job rotation and to plan optimum times and locations.

ii. *Reading Lists*. Planned reading gives a manager an opportunity to contribute to his own development, in his own time. It requires somebody to identify which books will be of value to the manager concerned and to discuss problems and concepts to ensure they are fully understood.

iii. *Special projects*. Quite apart from his normal job, a manager can be given a special project which will help him to develop. In a steel works a manager who was notoriously lax on safety was asked to make a study of the company's accident rate, safety methods and organisation and to make recommendations. He was given the opportunity to visit other works, provided with literature and given time to make the study on a part-time basis. At the end of the project he had not only produced an excellent report but—more important—he had changed his own attitude to safety.

iv. *Committee membership*. A planned period on a committee can also serve to extend a man, especially if he has some responsibility such as Chairman or Secretary.

v. *Attendance at Conferences*. This is useful if used in moderation and properly planned.
The reason why the man has been sent should be made clear and he should prepare a short report for his superior on the implications of the conference papers etc. for his department or company.

d. *Concentrate on 'on-the-job' training*.

Something like 90 per cent of a manager's development in knowledge, skills and attitudes occurs on the job.

Systematic guidance by his superior and the creation of the right kind of environment is necessary for success. There is no better way of bridging the gap between present and desired performance, for as L.F. Urwick puts it (33)

"Doing jobs well, being encouraged to do jobs that are a little outside what he believes to be his strength and then succeeding at them is a major influence on a man's development."

Even when a manager is sent on a course to broaden his outlook or teach him a new technique, this must complement what happens day-by-day in practice and cannot substitute for it.

There are some disadvantages. The superior may set a bad example: "Practice makes perfect but if we practise wrong, it comes out perfectly wrong". Coaching can be more apparent than real unless through Performance and Potential Review there is a systematic means of identifying what is needed. Finally, this method alone is unlikely to offer a complete solution since the superior is himself limited in knowledge and experience. If used alone it can cause in-breeding and narrowness.

e. *Build on strengths.*

Training is often regarded in a negative way as 'overcoming' a manager's weaknesses. Whilst this is useful it may prove more profitable to the company and the man to concentrate on building further his demonstrated strengths and abilities.

f. *Use internal training courses.*

Needs analysis often shows that a number of managers have common training requirements. It may be economic and efficient to teach them together on a course. Internal courses can be particularly helpful. They can be tailor-made to the proven needs of the individuals attending; time tables and travelling can be flexible for job demands; the contribution of company managers to the lectures and discussions gives them reality and relevance. The objectives of an internal course must be precisely stated, and the quality of presentation, imaginative use of case material, visual aids and so on must all be high.

g. *Use outside courses.*

An internal course can rarely meet all a company's needs. For example a man's outlook can be broadened when he attends courses where he mixes with people from other businesses and functions. An outside course on the practice of management can be a helpful framework for young men moving into management positions. Advanced teaching on the inter-relationship of functions, finance and market problems may be useful to those taking over general management roles for the first time. It is difficult to distinguish the good from the bad courses. A personal visit gives quick insight into the quality and background of the instructors, teaching material and physical facilities. In some countries the informal exchange of experience between companies is being strengthened by the establishment of a clearing-house of information. The British Institute of Management, among others, now provides such a service. Before any manager attends an outside course his boss should ask:

— Why is he going?

— What precisely do we expect him to get out of it?

— Will the company get a better result by sending a team instead of an individual?

— Have we been discriminating in our choice of course?

— Is the man briefed?

— What kind of report will he be asked to write?

— What plans do we have for follow-up when he returns?

Companies which have disciplined themselves to answer these questions before sending a man away on a course have been impressed by the benefits.

h. *Train for the future as well as the present.*

Forward company plans should always include the creation of new knowledge and skills which will be required. One insurance company sent all managers on training courses with a computer manufacturer well before their computer was installed. When a textile mill decided to re-equip with a new type of automatic loom, the Weaving Manager spent some months in the U.S.A. studying the managerial and technical implications of the equipment well before his looms were delivered.

A forward training plan must also flow from the company succession plans so that there are sufficient numbers of capable managers for the future demands of the business.

i. *Evaluate the results of training.*

Whilst it is difficult and in some cases impossible to evaluate the results of training, recent studies (34, 35) in the U.S.A. and Europe suggest that the effort is worthwhile. The discipline of establishing from the beginning just what changes training is required to achieve, often stems from the awareness that evaluation is going to be attempted. Even where evaluation, in terms of 'what impact did it have on the manager's performance and behaviour?', is limited, much can be learnt about the content, methods and presentation of the training so that it can be improved next time.

As with all the other techniques we are discussing, training can only make its full contribution if it is part of the total process of improving performance. In isolation, it achieves little and may even be injurious to the business. The classic warning is contained in a study of a series of management training courses carried out in a company in the United Kingdom. These courses were professionally well conducted and welcomed by the staff who attended but unfortunately top management was not itself deeply involved in the training. It is reported (36) that the company:

'... did achieve participant attitude change but found that the new attitudes conflicted with the practices of top management.

This conflict brought about serious organization strife, disagreement, frustration and even embitterment. Of the 97 supervisors who took the course, 19 left the company and another 25 sought other positions. Of those who had contact with top management, 80 per cent became dissatisfied. 83 per cent of those who took the course said it was a failure because it did not change top management attitudes! The dissatisfied group (those who either left the company or sought other employment) included nearly all the best qualified and most intelligent of the supervisors.

3. Salary structure and review.

So far we have been concerned with such non-financial incentives as job satisfaction, recognition of skill, sense of purpose and achievement. Whilst these are of great value in securing better performance the influence of financial rewards is also

100

significant as tangible evidence to the manager that his contribution is recognised. Moreover, financial rewards are a source of freedom from insecurity and the means by which the manager can improve the living standard of himself and his family.

Although many companies regard salary structure as a routine part of administration or a cost from which little benefit is derived, the true objectives of a progressive salary structure are far wider and should include the company's wish to:

— Attract and retain the numbers and quality of managers needed by the company.

— Reward managers equitably in relation to their personal contribution to the business, to each other and to their subordinates.

— Stimulate managers to perform better and not merely reward them for past services.

— Maintain a sensible relationship with salaries offered by comparable companies in the same job group/geographical location.

— Be economic and flexible in operating the structure, not mechanistic and bureaucratic.

There is no "one best structure" for rewarding managers and the many factors which can influence its shape can be illustrated by the following cases:

— Top management own the business and are interested in growth in share value rather than maximising base salaries.

— A company is expanding rapidly and as promotion prospects abound, a conservative base salary policy still attracts talented and ambitious people.

— The management group is ageing and more interested in deferred compensation in the form of pensions etc. than cash benefits in the current year.

— An unprofitable company in a declining industry can not afford to reward its managers generously. Ironically, it is forced to pay exceptionally high rewards in order to attract a few outstanding people from outside the industry into senior positions.

101

— A multi-national corporation believes in stock option plans as a potent means of identifying the interest of the business with that of the senior managers. Such schemes work well in the U.S.A. but tax considerations have since 1966 made them virtually useless in Great Britain.

— A large group organised into separate businesses finds it easier to relate individual bonus to profit contribution than a similar group organised on a centralised, functional basis.

— In some businesses and institutions, managers up to a very senior level are organised into unions which negotiate salaries and conditions for their members. Freedom to decide on structure is less in these circumstances than where it is top management's prerogative alone.

— Companies have vastly different "philosophies" which influence salary structures. One company may be tough and competitive in outlook with a high reward/high insecurity policy. Another may be conservative, paternalistic and stable where little is demanded from people and little given, apart from security.

These examples make it clear that every company must work out for itself the right "mix" of material rewards, which can range from base salary, bonuses, stock options, car, house, insurance, medical care, holidays, pensions and so on.

In spite of variations between countries and companies the base salary usually has the highest weighting in the total pattern of material rewards, often to the extent of 70% to 75%. The work done in the Improving Management Performance programme can be directly useful. One company found three factors to be relevant in deciding management job grades.

A primary factor of:

a. Contribution to business results (measured by Key Results Analysis).

and two secondary factors of:

b. Knowledge, skill and experience required (Measured by a Man Specification built up by stating for each Key Task what essential knowledge, skill, experience and qualification is required for satisfactory performance).

c. The "weight" of responsibility in terms of men, money, equipment and materials (measured by the first part of the Key Results Analysis).

The same company used the evidence from success or failure in securing Job Improvement Plans as a starting point for deciding on merit increases within the salary ranges, and for special bonuses.

The other important "weighting" in material rewards for the manager is additional financial bonus, which may be in the range of 15% to 20% of the total reward. Whilst the results of Job Improvement Plans provide some useful evidence great care is required in building up bonus schemes. For example, top management must consider where are bonus funds coming from? which managers are eligible? how often is bonus paid? how much? on what basis? Many so called scientific schemes do not in the long run provide the flexibility and realism which is required and become taken for granted. Certainly flexible and imaginative bonus schemes do focus attention on results and strengthen the link between company and individual goals.

4. Succession Plans.

The knowledge that there is a systematic approach to selection and succession planning within the company is also influential in building high morale. Over-preoccupation with promotion is frustrating but the company must have a:

Management inventory.

i.e. taking stock of the present group of managers, their experience, abilities, interests and how well they are performing in their present jobs is the essential "raw material" for planning management manpower. It is often imperfect in accuracy and limited in scope.

Succession plan.

i.e. relating the individual to the organization needs. This must be planned in depth since every move has a 'buffer impact' up and down the line and sometimes sideways. The selection methods must be effective to support the plan.

Career planning.

i.e. arranging the experience of managers so that they acquire the knowledge and skills for future posts which they might hold. This must take into consideration the manager's own ambitions and interests and not the company's view alone.

Succession planning can never be perfect. People leave unexpectedly, the 'high flier' reaches a plateau prematurely and the organization needs are changed by outside influences. However, it is just as necessary to have a five year, two year and next year plan in management manpower planning as it is for finance and markets. The failure to do this can be very serious because the 'lead time' required to build up a team of young men is perhaps in the order of ten years. Crash recruitment programmes forced on the company by an apparent shortage of talent within can damage the morale of existing managers.

Another common problem is the hoarding of talent within a Department or Unit as the manager seeks to achieve good operating results. This is easier for the Departmental Manager when he has a great deal of autonomy of authority to promote from his own staff, without also looking elsewhere in the company for other candidates and when he has significant authority to prevent one of his own men being transferred or promoted to another department. The company's overall interest in placing the right man in the right job is lost when succession plans are fragmented into many local "empires". It is necessary to establish for each manager the key task of creating men of talent and potential for the company and to take a company view of succession.

The Succession Plan is *quantitative:* how many people will we require to fill posts in the future, bearing in mind the company's plans for growth and our past experience of labour turnover?

In practice it is difficult to do this calculation and some companies are experimenting with the use of the computer to help them. An interesting by-product of the preparatory work in one Group was that subsidiary companies supposedly doing the same thing with common policies had quite different ratios of managers to capital employed and different criteria for judging future numbers.

104

The Succession Plan is also *qualitative:* "Even if we can get the numbers right, what new kinds of knowledge and skills will be required?" The explosive growth of science; the growing complexity of business; the developing international character of larger companies are typical of the factors which have to be considered.

It is clear that the bureaucratic answer to succession planning—"Promote the senior man"—which is surprisingly hard in dying will not be good enough in the future. Lyndall Urwick in a stimulating paper, "The value of eccentricity", (37) points out that a healthy business must have two types of manager:

— the faithful administrators who maintain the routine and keep the corporation in order and who try to stifle;
— the lunatics, eccentrics and initiators who are the source of new ideas and who are usually fighting procedures and tradition.

The Chief Executive has to find the right balance between these types at any one time. If the administrators kill off the lunatics the business will go bankrupt very, very slowly. If the lunatics get absolute power the business will go bankrupt at high speed. In most businesses the Chief Executive will find his main preoccupation is to nurture and protect the small number of eccentrics.

I. CONTINUITY.

Once the launching phase is complete, the role of the Adviser usually ends, although he may of course continue to be available for advice. His success can be measured by the extent to which the various techniques have become self-generating because they are really useful to managers.

A clear definition of responsibility for administration is required. For example, the Personnel Department may be authorised to issue Potential Review Forms.

A statement of policy is often valuable and it must be tailor-made for the company concerned, since the discussions about its content are as important as the final statement. One company's (38) policy is to:

1. Provide all managers and potential managers in General Electric (U.S.) with challenges and opportunities for maximum self-development on their present jobs and for advancement as earned.
2. To work towards improving skill and competence throughout the entire manager group so as to help General Electric managers to become equal to the demands of tomorrow's management job.
3. To operate to furnish the Company with both the number and kind of managers that will be needed in the years ahead.
4. To encourage systematic habits and procedures to make it simpler for each manager to discharge his manager development responsibility.

IV. COMMON PROBLEMS

A. ORGANISATION STRUCTURE.

Problems which impinge directly on company organisation structure inevitably arise as objectives and key results are thought through. After all, the structure itself exists only to facilitate the achievement of company and personal goals by grouping related activities, setting out clearly areas of key tasks and authority for results and clarifying the main formal working relationships.

It is true that a good formal organisation structure is ineffective if relationships are bad. Equally, a poor structure can be a serious obstacle to success in achieving results because it encourages friction and power politics, time consuming delays, unclear communication and wasteful effort by managers. No perfect, final structure ever exists. Every business inherits a legacy of personalities, emotions and habits which are hard to change and these informal relationships can be very influential. People break through over-rigid definitions and neat procedures as they seek to express individual and group drives and personality. As long as the main structure is soundly designed this challenge and variety is constructive and stimulating. It is wrong to imply however that good informal relationships are in themselves sufficient and to ignore the contribution which good organisation design can make. Every business is a living organism and its structure must be adjusted as the shape and purpose of the business alter.

Certainly the link between organization structure and Improving Management Performance is particularly important because the analysis of individual jobs only makes sense in the broader picture of the business structure. One management job has to be understood in relation to others. This is well summarized in the 'Objectives of the Glacier Project' (39) where it is stated that '... managerial effectiveness is partly a function of the personality and character of the manager. Training can do little to change these personal qualities. A manager's behaviour is, however, strongly influenced by the correctness of definition of the role he occupies, the relationship of this role to other roles and the total system, the terms of reference governing his role and the degrees to which the manager understands these matters. Modification and clarification of such conditions can, therefore, produce significant changes in managerial behaviour and effectiveness."

A National Industrial Conference Board survey (40) of 167 United States companies, made in 1964, refers to the 'increasingly close association of management development and organization planning. In many situations, these responsibilities are combined in one company unit: development is one of the responsibilities assigned to the organization planning unit: or less commonly, organization planning is assigned to the management development staff. These responsibilities are recognized as the two sides of one coin'.

1. Critical questions.

Looking at the organization structure in relation to company objectives and the Key Results Analyses some useful questions can be asked:

Is there an effective division of work to be done?

Is the division between functions sound?

Is there confusion between staff/line?

Are staff doing work which the line managers could do as easily?

8

What is the balance of power between H.Q. and the individual units?

Is it sound?

Is there scope for decentralisation to separate profit centres?

Is there proper provision for policy making as a separate activity from execution?

Looking at Managers:

What sort of decisions do they make themselves?

How important are these decisions?

How far do they have discretion and how far are decisions "programmed"?

Do their decisions have an impact beyond their own job?

What is the time span before someone checks up on the decision?

What is the urgency and frequency of decisions?

Do they delegate too much or too little?

Are responsibilities and objectives really understood?

Did Key Results Analysis show that managers really knew the results they were expected to achieve?

And that they could distinguish between important and unimportant elements in their work?

Do managers understand the role of others with whom they have a working relationship?

Is there a sound line of command?

Is there a clear line of direct authority from top to bottom?

Do functional links confuse or strengthen this?

How many management levels are there? Too many? A missing level?

What is the span of control—is it sound?

Is there provision for control and accountability?

Is there good control over Key Results Areas?

Are there gaps?

Is there a sound pattern of reporting, written and verbal?

Are controls at a frequency and in a form which help or impede good decision-making?

Does the organization provide for proper use of human resources?

Are managers doing tasks which should be delegated?

Or done by machine?

Are jobs too 'small' so that people can't grow?

Are jobs too 'big' so that they are done inefficiently?

Is there too much 'insurance' built into the organization —advisers, technical and specialist support etc.—so that the managers and supervisors really do not have a management job left?

Is the time spent in a job too long so that people get stale?

Or too short so that they never really master the job before they leave?

Is the structure working in good spirit?

Is there team collaboration in getting things done or is the operation autocratic?

Is the structure reasonably well understood and accepted?

Is it flexible and 'commonsense' in daily practice?

Or is it rigid and unable to adapt itself to long term needs?

Does it encourage delay and politics through lack of clarity?

Do people feel committed to and involved in the organisation's purpose?

2. Trends in organisation.

Whilst every business has to find its own answers to these questions some general trends are evident.

a. Delegation and the role of the Chief Executive.

Almost every Chief Executive confirms that he is over-pre-occupied with detail that ought to be carried by subordinates. The result is that his personal and undelegatable responsibilities get neglected. Thus a major emphasis in organisation change arising from an Improving Management Performance programme is a determined drive to delegate responsibility for results. The confidence to do so builds up as the work disciplines people to

— clarify precisely what responsibility and authority for results is delegated;

— strengthen control data so that feedback of significant variance is improved;

— improve the competence and knowledge of managers so that they are able to accept more responsibility;

— build up a sense of team and personal enthusiasm in getting results.

Without these things, saying "we must delegate better" is only a pious platitude.

Once the Chief Executive delegates in a positive way it extends down the business.

Having relieved the detailed load, what are the things with which the Chief Executive is still concerned? Two quotations illustrate this:

When Lord Cole, Chairman of Unilever, was asked by *The Observer* how he spends his time he replied (41):

"Well, apart from such general questions as morale, public relations and where the money is coming from I suppose it boils down to three or four things; the annual operating plan; capital expenditure; selection and pay of our top managers; and the new roads along which Unilever should travel in the future."

Ralph J. Cordiner, formerly Chairman of American General Electric Company and its Chief Executive Officer, discussing the responsibility of the chief executive said (42):

"He should first of all generate with his associates what I call a "vision of the business". That is to say he should not only have a clear picture of the business as it stands today, but, more importantly, a vision of what he wants it to be in ten or twenty years in the future." ... "he then has the responsibility to organise all the resources of the company in order to make his programme a profitable reality. This involves the specific work of establishing objectives, policies and plans for the business and an organisation that can effectively carry them out. It also involves winning the understanding and willing co-operation of associates at all levels, so that they will do their part voluntarily and creatively and this communication duty is most important."

b. Decentralisation.

The wish to delegate often leads large businesses to decentralise a complex functional organisation into smaller units, preferably capable of being treated as profit centres.

The precise shape of such decentralisation into product grouping, geographical grouping or a mixture of the two requires careful study. An Improving Business Results programme coupled with decentralisation can have a dramatically favourable impact on profits as "administrators" are persuaded to think and act as "entrepreneurs." Traditionally parochial attitudes give way to a more commercial, general management outlook. Decisions can be made on site that used to have to go to the centre. The problem of high level succession is eased as there develops a wider number of people who have been tested by having to run a business.

Decentralisation, like delegation, has become a fashionable word. Its virtues are evident but before undertaking it on a large scale various issues require study:

company strengths and weaknesses; forward objectives; building up enough men competent to take over at the launching stage; making sure that controls are effective so that the contribution and difficulties of the new profit centre can be monitored; watching the size of the decentralised units so that the overhead burden does not get out of hand as each unit sets up its own functional and service functions.

c. Tighter central control.

This may appear contradictory to the trend towards decentralisation. Most successful decentralised businesses have appreciated that matters such as major capital investment are so important that the centre must control them. A new breed of highly professional corporate staff men is emerging, small

111

in number but high in quality. They help the Chief Executive to formulate policies and to monitor the progress of divisions. The ability of the centre to exercise control is being increased by:

— the more thorough and precise way in which Divisional forward objectives and plans are analysed and presented. Standards of Divisional performance are clearer and it is more obvious to the centre when variances occur;
— the development of mathematical techniques and the computer now makes it desirable to take an overall group view of some problems, which previously would not have been possible.

A total view of stock levels, warehouse location and customer service is one example. Another, is an oil company where the arrival of tankers, various crude oils, the possibility of producing different blends, geographical location of refineries and so on have to be matched with customer demand. A company, rather than a refinery view is likely to be more profitable. This means that the discretion of the local Refinery Manager is being reduced.

Looking ahead, the policy of some banks to link their main branches by computer to the centre can be expected to reduce the branch manager's responsibility for making loans.

B. CONTROLS.

Financial budgets and controls are of great value, since money is a 'universal' measure and one which ultimately indicates company success or failure. Moreover, it is only when managers' suggestions, alternative courses of action, changes in government policies and so on are considered both in their own right and in their complex inter-relationships in money terms that a sound judgment of priorities can be made. For example, a Sales Director makes a case out for price reduction in a certain product and supports the proposal with a forecast increase in volume. It requires a complex financial analysis to see whether *overall* this is likely to be profitable for the company. Managers recognise the need for this kind of information and a survey made by the British Institution of Works Managers (43) showed that managers complained that they had "insufficient cost information to indicate the best areas for improvement in productivity."

Equally important is the managers' need for information in *non-financial terms as well,* if he is to be helped to make quick and sound decisions. Some guidelines in this field are:

1. Guidelines.

a. Focus on vital results.

The first priority is to establish control over the key results of a job. This can lead to an economy in paper work, as information about unimportant matters is discontinued, but its real value is in creating a new attitude of mind.

In discussing earlier the problem of how to identify Key Results it was said that a relatively small number of results will govern success substantially: "the 80/20 rule." This same concept is profitably employed to control data itself. For example, 58% of the cost of manufacturing Product X arose from expensive raw materials. Thus the most detailed and timely control information on material utilisation etc. was fed to managers daily. The remaining 42% of cost was spread over a dozen different areas: some justified weekly data, others only an occasional sample check. As Drucker writes (44):

'The real difficulty lies indeed not in determining what objectives we need, but in deciding how to set them. There is only one fruitful way to make this decision: by determining what shall be measured in each area and what the yardstick of measurement should be.

For the measurement used determines what one pays attention to... It makes things visible and tangible. The things included in the measurement become relevant; the things omitted are out of sight and mind.'

b. Are simple and relevant.

Imaginative study is required to ensure that the management control data supplied to a manager is in terms he understands, is relevant for good decision making and compels him to pay attention to the basic company purpose. In practice a mass of control data often builds up insidiously, much of it pointless and costly to produce, until managers are virtually paralysed

113

by the sheer weight of information. As the old adage has it: "The art of boredom is to tell all."

Management by exception becomes extremely difficult and a curious situation can develop where a manager gives up the unequal task of studying the available data and starts to interfere at lower levels, or initiates "special studies," to try to find out what is really happening.

An article in "Management Today" (45) describes how Marks and Spencers Ltd., the respected British retail chain, handles this problem. They found, for example, that in one operation it cost £6. to check an average error of 1/11d. In their search for simplicity and relevance they set no targets for the stores in terms of profit performance; only in turnover. The control system of the company is designed to focus attention on its basic purpose: "All stock is counted not in numbers but in retail value. All budgets are drawn up in retail sales, like all targets. When it comes to setting these, says a director, 'we're really very simple'—almost unbelievably so. 'The only yardstick we really apply is the increase in volume.' Look after the sales, in other words, and, provided costs are not allowed to escalate, the profits will look after themselves."

c. Stimulate action.

The control report should signal clearly to the manager that there is a variance from the agreed plan, of sufficient magnitude to justify investigation. Note that variance does not only mean "failing to meet target" for it can just as well show an unexpected success which could be exploited by follow-through action.

Some companies find it useful to distinguish between variances within the control of the individual manager and those out of his control.

d. Encourage self-direction.

If the basic philosophy has been followed, the individual manager has contributed to and is now completely clear what results he must achieve. These results are the "standard," variances from which will be shown by controls.

He will therefore welcome control data as a real help to

114

achieving his own goals. If this sounds platitudinous consider how many managers regard control as a tool for their boss to "catch them out" and therefore divert a considerable amount of ingenuity and effort to "making the figures look right." The climate of opinion and the actual use of a control form is as significant as the layout and design of the form. Different levels require different kinds of information for their self direction and this is illustrated in Exhibit 14 which shows the hierarchy of control for contract managers in a construction company.

2. Trends in controls.

Certainly control problems are amongst the most persistent and complex ones to be faced. At present a great deal of research and re-thinking is apparent as top management seeks to measure better what it knows to be critical. Ralph Cordiner of American General Electric Company in his book, (46) 'New Frontiers for Professional Managers' writes:

'it is an immense problem to organize and communicate the information required to operate a large, decentralized organization... What is required... is... a penetrating and orderly study of the business in its entirety to discover what specific information is needed at each particular position in view of the decisions to be made there...'

Dean Stanley F. Teele of the Harvard Business School supports this view when he says (47) of the future:

'I think the capacity to manage knowledge will be still more important to the manager... The manager will need to increase his skill in deciding what knowledge he needs.'

Some of the practical problems we are currently meeting are:

— the continued use of a static information pattern when the business is itself changing rapidly, for example through decentralization, growth, diversification, new technology;
— uncertainty about the cost of securing information in relation to the potential benefits it will bring;
— a narrow view of control, for example, the absence of control data about the market environment in which the business operates;

115

EXHIBIT 14

**HIERARCHY OF CONTROL
FOR CONTRACT MANAGEMENT
IN A CONSTRUCTION COMPAN**

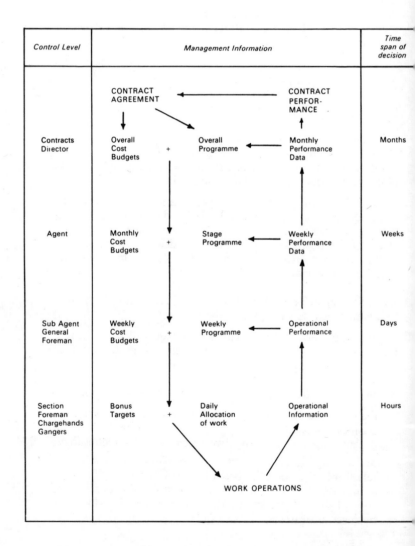

Control Level	Management Information				Time span of decision
	CONTRACT AGREEMENT			CONTRACT PERFOR-MANCE	
Contracts Director	Overall Cost Budgets	+	Overall Programme	Monthly Performance Data	Months
Agent	Monthly Cost Budgets	+	Stage Programme	Weekly Performance Data	Weeks
Sub Agent General Foreman	Weekly Cost Budgets	+	Weekly Programme	Operational Performance	Days
Section Foreman Chargehands Gangers	Bonus Targets	+	Daily Allocation of work	Operational Information	Hours
			WORK OPERATIONS		

— the belief that financial budgetary control is enough;

— 'technical' problems of measurement.

Encouraging progress is being made as we learn to make better use of computers and the wider implications of this are dealt with more fully later in this book. Better management performance depends greatly on our capacity to measure and inform, so that self control can be exercised by the individual, particularly in relation to his key results. Seventy-six years ago Lord Kelvin presented a similar challenge (48): 'When you can measure what you are speaking about, and express it in numbers, you know something about it. But when you cannot measure it, when you cannot express it in numbers, your knowledge is of a meagre and unsatisfactory kind.'

PART FOUR

LAUNCHING AN IMPROVING BUSINESS RESULTS PROGRAMME

By now, a Chief Executive may be saying to himself: "I can see some value in this approach although I certainly do not think *all* the techniques are appropriate for my business. Anyway, in some of the areas discussed I think we are already doing a sound job. Where in practice *do* I make a start?"

The only really satisfactory way to answer this question is to make a study of each business and its unique needs, problems, personalities and present methods. There is no "package deal," for as L. F. Urwick warns us (49), a business cannot solve its problems merely by buying a technique or system:

'Every business enterprise is a living organism, with its own traditions, its own climate of opinion, its own special make-up. Every situation is different. And every kind of system has to be custom-built to the individual business.'

We should consider five fundamental requirements for successful launching:

A. UNDERSTANDING BY TOP MANAGEMENT.
B. A PERCEPTIVE PRELIMINARY STUDY AND LAUNCHING PLAN.
C. HIGH QUALITY TRAINING OF ADVISERS AND OTHER SPECIALISTS.
D. SUSTAINED ATTACK.
E. SPECIAL CARE IN CO-ORDINATING LONG RANGE AND SHORT TERM PLANS.

A. UNDERSTANDING BY TOP MANAGEMENT.

Improving Business Results is a searching way to manage a business not just a tool for the planner or the personnel manager.

Programmes launched without the involvement and understanding of the top management team have an odds on chance of ending as "interesting experiments."

The Chief Executive must lead the project and give it the support of his knowledge, authority and example, and this leadership can only come from a deep conviction that the programme is worthwhile. The Chief Executive could usefully take his senior

119

managers to appreciation seminars run by such institutions as Management Centre Europe. The American Management Association runs sessions throughout the U.S.A. and in Britain seminars are provided by British Institute of Management and the Urwick Management Centre.

These seminars provide an opportunity to explore practical problems more fully, to hear case histories, to rub shoulders with other top managers, both "converts" and "sceptics." It may also be possible, through an introduction from one of the Management Institutes to visit a company which has had practical experience so that a first hand account of difficulties and benefits can be obtained. Personal discussions with specialists in this field may be fruitful.

B. A PERCEPTIVE PRELIMINARY STUDY AND LAUNCHING PLAN.

Having decided to go ahead the next question is where to start. A preliminary study should be made covering such facts as the overall financial state of the company; its present organisation structure; current objectives and how they are set; present methods of defining a manager's results; the scope and technique of controls; current techniques of appraisal, training, identification of potential and succession planning. The attitude of mind and morale of managers and the pressures to which they are subjected should also be assessed. The scope of a preliminary study will reflect the major problems facing the business.

This background information makes it possible to decide the best launching sequence. There is no standard pattern to be copied and the range of choice can be illustrated from our consultant casebook:

Company A:

This company was very worried about training and developing managers for the future. They had first planned to send them on courses but then decided that Improving Management Performance would be a better approach. They were quite confident that company objectives were clear and needed no examination so the initial effort was concentrated on managers from the Foreman up to the Works Manager and key results analysis and improvement plans were used to get better results. Performance and potential review then enabled the company to establish training schemes and prepare its succession plans.

For top management this work had an unexpected effect. Their managers challenged unit objectives, saying they were unrealistic and unenterprising and several hundred constructive suggestions for improvements in controls, standards, performance of machines, material usage and so on were made. Gaps and overlaps in company policy were revealed. Top management found themselves stimulated to re-think critically their company plans and they began to look much more systematically at the outside environment and to plan for longer periods ahead.

Company B:

Company B was dissatisfied with its rate of return on assets and felt that their attempts to see the forward trend had been too casual and short term. They determined to subject themselves to a critical study, looking at their own strengths and weaknesses and the threat of growing competition. They set up a sub-committee of the Main Board and assigned to it a special Long Range Planning team of three people. An outside consultant advised the group.

Executive management, with help from this team brought about major changes in the company. An unprofitable Canadian subsidiary was sold; the organisation was decentralised; a market research section was established. A company 3-year plan was created which set out to achieve a 5% improvement in return on net assets. The company is currently engaged in a detailed Improving Management Performance programme in order to get accountability and motivation down to every level of management.

Company C:

In this large Group of companies the Group Managing Director, the Managing Director of X Division and the Personnel Director investigated personally a number of other companies which had used the Improving Management Performance approach. They determined to introduce it into their Group. They called together the General Managers of X Division and, with outside help,

9

ran a one day appreciation seminar. Afterwards they asked for "volunteers" to carry out a pilot project. One company was finally selected, a thorough survey was made and a plan of campaign prepared. In this case the starting point was a rigorous examination of unit objectives and their link with company objectives, and the improvement of management performance. Their team of Advisers consisted of high quality men loaned from other Divisions as well as Division X. In this way Advisers were ready trained to lead the work in their home Divisions as soon as results were secured from the pilot work. Thus from a deep but small scale project the Group got better financial results, and both confidence and competent men for rapid expansion of the work. Problems relating to overall Group policy in turn led to a reappraisal of the Group's 5 year Plan.

Company D:

The President of this multi-national Group took a different view which was confirmed by careful survey. It was to risk the dangers of dilution in quality, and attack simultaneously on a wide front embracing many companies in different countries. The focal point was to be on local company unit objectives and manager development. A high quality central Adviser Team was set up and they in turn trained an Adviser in each company. They were able to establish quickly an attitude of mind that it was possible to set objectives and to begin to plan for improvement; to identify hidden talent in the group; to set the scene for a second phase of work in which financial controls, one and five year company plans were introduced.

Company E:

This company faced a crisis situation and losses were mounting. The new Chairman concentrated on really fundamental issues: what was the company trying to achieve? what business were they really in? what were the immediate threats? A marketing study showed the need to change the company's selling approach in a significant way. Other studies showed scope for major cost reduction. The top organisation structure and many senior managers had to be changed and new, stringent controls established. Clearly this was no time for refined key results analysis when the nature of jobs was in the melting pot and simpler statements supported by improvement plans were more appropriate. In the midst of these urgent measures, the com-

122

pany gave a senior manager specific responsibility for working on management development for the future.

These cases are different in many ways yet they have in common the Chief Executive's recognition of the unity underlying the techniques.

Some dangers to avoid when deciding on the best launching sequence include:

— setting up a Long Range Planning department which operates as an "academic exercise" with line operating managers not involved and with no formal link established between forward planning and current operational planning;

— assigning poor quality or inexperienced people to the work. If it is worth doing at all it requires the best talents in the business. The willingness of a Chief Executive to spare a valuable man is usually the best test of his seriousness of intent;

— inadequate training and guidance for the Advisers and other specialists involved;

— fragmenting effort, for example by doing Key Results Analysis for individuals instead of for a management team from top to bottom. Or by working horizontally across the business dealing, say, with all foremen when the line of command through which results must be achieved is necessarily a vertical one;

— failure to plan for regular critical reviews at which results can be monitored.

C. HIGH QUALITY TRAINING OF ADVISERS AND OTHER SPECIALISTS.

There are three interlocking training problems. First, the need to train a Company Adviser who will help top management to launch the Improving Management Performance work, which includes clarifying unit objectives. In an earlier section we have stressed the importance of having a man of high quality, preferably with line management background, assigned to the project. When the launching is over he is not normally required because managers should themselves be undertaking the work as their normal way of getting business results. Some residual procedures (e.g. potential review) can be handled by existing departments (e.g. personnel department). It is very important to train Advisers to the highest professional standards in the knowledge and experience which has now been developed into a coherent and teachable form. For example, they should know how to help a manager to make a Key Results Analysis; understand new techniques of performance and potential review; be able to analyse training needs and so on. The best way to learn to be an Adviser is by on-the-job tuition in theory and guided practice, and larger companies have invariably used this method for training their Advisers. To satisfy a national need in Great Britain a new service for training Advisers from small companies will soon be available.

The second training problem is to develop men who are permanently or temporarily working in the Long Range Planning group. The range of disciplines needed is so wide that a great deal must be learnt on the job whilst a member of teams studying complex problems. These men should be given a total view of the nature of long range planning at an early stage and short seminars are helpful when supported by guided reading.

The third training problem relates to the managers who are involved in the programme. They are given a full explanation of the programme, why it was launched and the objectives to be reached. At each new phase of the programme detailed guidance and discussion opportunities should be provided. In the Improving Management Performance work there is no substitute for personal counselling on the job for each individual manager if high quality results are to be obtained.

D. SUSTAINED ATTACK.

Done well, the Improving Management Performance aspect of the programme brings measurable and worthwhile short term improvements. Sometimes this success creates an air of inevitability that improvements will continue at the same rate and that attention can be turned to new matters. Nothing is further from the truth. The early work, though rewarding, nearly always throws up problems of a company nature which cannot be solved quickly, e.g. the need to find a new product to replace one which though doing well now is showing signs of future decline. All these problems, threats and opportunities, should form part of the study of the company's strategic considerations.

124

Sustained attack is necessary for another reason. It is rare to find a situation where the managers cannot find improvement areas, and get results... the first time round. Next time, it gets harder and the initial excitement wears thin. During the second and third year after launching, the Chief Executive must, by example and drive, ensure that what is launched continues to grow and develop. Old habits and attitudes are not always changed quickly. It takes time and perseverance to get the programme so thoroughly embedded into the business that it ceases to be a "programme" or a new project and becomes "the way we run our company."

The same determination must support the long range planning activity and the organisation and staffing must be appropriate. The choice is wide. For example, in a recent study of the organisational needs or trends of European and American multi-national companies George Steiner points out (50) that no single best organisation exists. The pattern includes:

"1. A full-time planning executive in company headquarters and a full-time planning executive in each of the major operating divisions and subsidiaries.

2. A corporate worldwide planning executive at world headquarters but no clearly defined planning executives at operational levels.

3. A planning executive in major operating units but no central planning group or single executive solely responsible for planning at central headquarters.

4. The location of the planning function within one of the major functional areas (such as finance, marketing, product planning) to serve as a formal focus of all corporate planning.

5. No formal planning organisation at all even though a good bit of planning takes place in the management of the company."

This study suggest that most large multi-national companies have established staff units of specialists to help top management, and very often there is a vice-president in charge of all types of planning.

E. SPECIAL CARE IN CO-ORDINATING LONG AND SHORT TERM PLANS.

Intellectually there is no problem since strategic and tactical plans set the framework and priorities in which meaningful unit objectives are established and from which, in turn, individual managers derive their priorities. A practical difficulty may come from separation between Long Range Planners and Operational Managers. The former group is usually the Company's most senior management with a man or group acting as specialist staff adviser. By definition these specialists are looking a long way ahead and thinking particularly about the outside environmental changes which might occur. They get "growth" minded and may feel it wiser to "have another look" before crystallising their recommendations. Operational Managers say that they are also interested in the future, but the sheer pressure under which they have to work to get short term results in fact dominates their thinking. On the whole they are compelled to look inside the organisation at the short term crises and difficulties that really won't wait. They talk more about efficiency than growth.

In one company the Long Range Planning group proposed that a much higher proportion of a major product should be exported. It was a wise recommendation in view of the group's long term strategy to make themselves less dependent on the United Kingdom market. The Sales Manager accepted the logic but was strikingly slow to follow through. He felt that this was a diversion from the immediate job of selling in the home market and it could have a detrimental effect on his results there. Although he would not have admitted it, he felt insecure about his capacity to cope with an unknown new set of problems such as tariffs, quotas, languages, etc.

Of course there are solutions to such problems. It is essential for people in this position to be deeply concerned with the initial study and determination of policy. The general point is that special attention is needed to ensure that strategic and operation planning really do link together practically and emotionally.

It would seem logical to launch every programme by establishing Strategic and Tactical Plans and then moving on to unit and individual objectives. However, it is not unusual for

126

a company to start with Improving Management Performance and clarifying unit short term objectives, identifying important cost reductions and other improvements, creating enthusiasm for achieving results through key results analysis, improvement plans, performance reviews and training.

Once this work is well under way valuable data about the company's strengths and weaknesses is available for the long range planning work. And there is an assurance that when new plans *are* created there will be a more purposeful and able team to get the results. Equally important, most managers at present feel themselves inextricably trapped in the rat-race of today's problems. Only when some of these problems are solved can managers find the time and energy to think deeply about the potential of tomorrow's business.

PART FIVE

WIDER
IMPLICATIONS

It is useful to stand back from detailed techniques and comment on some of the wider implications stemming from "Improving Business Results."

A. THE IMPORTANCE OF THE CHIEF EXECUTIVE.
B. A DEEPER UNDERSTANDING OF HUMAN MOTIVATION.
C. THE DEVELOPMENT OF COMPUTERS AND MATHEMATICAL TOOLS.

A. THE IMPORTANCE OF THE CHIEF EXECUTIVE.

In our concern for building teamwork and a shared sense of purpose it should not be forgotten that the personal courage and leadership of the Chief Executive is of critical importance. Often he initiates a programme of work when, in the early stages, there is reserve and scepticism amongst his colleagues. The final act of business judgement, when all the analyses and alternatives are set down, is his. Certainly he has to lead his colleagues in re-thinking the objectives of the business. He must develop a genuine sense of participation amongst his managers and be receptive to their constructive criticism. By example, he must concentrate on accomplishment and be willing to delegate and encourage risk taking.

It does not follow that personal leadership is the *only* requirement, nor that the Chief Executive is an entirely free agent to do with the business what he wills. In a true and lasting sense the Chief Executive's leadership within his business is educational in generating purposefulness, creativity and a commitment to the company goals amongst his team. One of his most important responsibilities is the appointment of managers, particularly to senior positions. Obviously the candidate's qualifications in terms of his past record of securing results and his knowledge and experience will be influential; so will the man's personal acceptability to his colleagues. Just as important is the man's integrity. It is no accident that in Peter Drucker's classic "Practice of Management" he keeps repeating this word, insisting that "the best practices will fail to breed the right spirit unless management bears witness for its own professed beliefs every time it appoints a man to a management job. The final proof of its sincerity and seriousness is uncompromising emphasis on integrity of character... in appointing people to top positions integrity cannot be over-emphasised. In fact, no one should be appointed unless management is willing to have his character serve as the model for all his subordinates."

The Chief Executive's responsibility for leadership in relation to the environment in which the business lives, is no less important. Levitt refers to (51) "... a vision that can produce eager followers in vast numbers. In business, the followers are customers. To produce these customers, the entire corporation must be viewed as a customer creating and customer satisfying organism. Management must think of itself not as producing products but as providing customer-creating value satisfaction." "And the Chief Executive himself has the inescapable responsibility of creating this environment, this viewpoint, this attitude, this aspiration."

In a broader context the Chief Executive must get his colleagues to recognise that economic decisions and policies often have a social and community influence. For example, a management training and promotion programme open to all men of ability is good business management. The same programme makes a more subtle social contribution in breaking down class barriers and nepotism. There is a challenging and constructive role for business in contributing to the development of this society of which it is an integral part.

B. A DEEPER UNDERSTANDING OF HUMAN MOTIVATION.

Built unobtrusively into our practical techniques are perceptions about human motivation and needs derived from social science research. The word "unobtrusively" needs stressing at present. Social sciences are becoming fashionable with the result that managers are sometimes exposed to a new "mystique," with its jargon and high priests. Taught in this way practical managers may treat the subject as though it were another "fad"—interesting, stimulating, worth a minor experiment but in the last resort rather a luxury and not directly concerned with effective business management. This attitude is wrong, but it is understandable. Whilst some teaching and development of self-perception about management style is useful, the major challenge is to build this valuable thinking in a natural and simple way into business management. For example, the deep involvement of the managers is secured by:

— briefing sessions;
— team studies of objectives and areas for improvement;
— key results analysis where manager, boss and superior of the boss are involved;
— action plans for improvement, where the three levels are involved;
— performance and potential review, where three levels of management are involved;
— identifying training needs where the man's own perception of his needs is always significant;
— involving the man in self-development and making him primarily responsible for seeing that the company training plan for him is carried out;
— getting the man to create and use control information for his personal control.

Similarly, where it is appropriate, groups of managers who have a direct influence on a problem or plan of action work together and these groups are often built up from a diagonal slice of the organisation or from a blend of functional and operational interests.

Salary structure and working conditions are important but there is a deeper motivation when a man is an active agent in his own change; is committed to goals; has insight into his own style of management and higher competence at building inter-personal and group relationships.

The striking characteristic of the "Improving Business Results" approach is the way in which it unleashes contribution and enthusiasm, supporting the view of the late Douglas McGregor that: (52)

"The expenditure of physical and mental effort in work is as natural as play or rest.
External control and the threat of punishment are not the only means for bringing about effort towards organizational

objectives. Man will exercise self-control in the service of the objectives to which he is committed. Commitment to objectives is dependent on the rewards associated with their achievement. The most important rewards are those that satisfy needs for self-respect and personal improvement. The average human being learns, under proper conditions, not only to accept but to seek responsibility.

The capacity to exercise a relatively high degree of imagination, ingenuity, and creativity in the solution of organizational problems is widely, not narrowly, distributed in the population. Under the conditions of modern industrial life, the intellectual potentialities of the average human being are only partially utilized."

This is a completely different outlook from those who believe that managers resent and resist a demanding environment. "Improving Business Results" *is* demanding since it is focussed on results and concerned with measurable benefits for manager and company, not with vague generalisation and platitude. It is not enough to agree what a man must do, but rather to define what he must achieve; not enough to analyse a problem, but rather to produce an action plan to begin to solve it; not enough to issue instructions but to associate with them measures of accountability with a firm completion date.

Looking at tomorrow's opportunities rather than yesterday's mistakes demands flexibility in ensuring that the company's human, physical and financial resources are concentrated in the areas of greatest opportunity. It may be thought that this insistence on measurable results will arouse antagonism in managers, because it could make them more vulnerable to criticism. The opposite is true, in practice, for most managers wish to be judged fairly against an agreed set of standards. As William Whyte wrote: (53)

"No one likes to be played checkers with, and the man the Organisation needs most is precisely the man who is most sensitive on this point. To control one's destiny and not to be controlled by it; to know which way the path will fork and to make the turning oneself; to have some index of achievement that no one can dispute—concrete and tangible for all to see— not dependent on the attitude of others. It is an independence he will never have in full measure but he must forever seek it."

132

C. DEVELOPMENT OF COMPUTERS AND MATHEMATICAL TOOLS.

The development of computers and mathematical tools is now recognised as revolutionary in its impact on management. The approach to Improving Business Results described so far has imperfectly sought to encourage fundamental attitudes, such as:

— Managers must think about the dynamic "whole" of the business and not just try to improve isolated elements.

— Cold-blooded, critical and factual analysis is necessary before using human judgement to weigh alternative courses of action.

— Feedback of results to each manager and to the business generally is essential if corrective action is to be taken.

Some of the new tools are already well proved in helping managers make better decisions. Take, for example, the problem facing top management of the Wiggins Teape paper group in Britain: (54) they recognised that a major new integrated paper mill at Fort William in Scotland would make necessary a revision of the methods of distributing paper from the point of manufacture to the customer. In particular it was felt that a policy of central warehousing might improve customer service and reduce distribution and production costs. In the past, paper from 16 mills went to 12 branch warehouses; orders up to 1 ton would be delivered directly to customers from branches; orders over 1 ton would be delivered directly to customers from mills. In making the "best decision" for the future in terms of service and cost, management had to consider such control variables as the number of storage points; the location of these storage points; the quantity of stocks to be held in each storage point; the various methods of distribution available from the production units and the random variable of the total demand for paper, say in the next 6 months. A multi-discipline project team developed Distribution and Production Mathematical Models, and used the computer for simulation and provided top management with the following facts:

No. of Central Warehouses	1 CW	2 CW	3 CW
Service improved by	3 days	7 days	7 days
Mills productivity improved by	7%	7%	Less than 5%
Transport cost	up 2%	down 10%	down 16%
Stockholding cost	down 4%	up 14%	up 32%

The best business balance between customer service and transport, stockholding and production costs would be realised by establishing 2 central warehouses with the primary function of holding all mill stocks.

This is typical of the way in which management's capacity to make better decisions is being aided by mathematical tools and the computer at present. Clearly today's managers in every type and size of business must gain a fuller appreciation of these tools, even where they do not have specialists or their own computer. A small chain of grocery and hardware stores with 80 branches was also worried about inventory problems. The collection of sample data and the use of an existing computer programme for sales forecasting and stock control showed a saving of £ 30,000 in the total inventory. The cost of the computer time was £ 25. Or take the problem facing a construction company: what was the optimum work schedule for placing 20,000 lorry loads of material at 120 different work areas of a one mile square site in a stated time. The mathematics are simple, but the calculations so overwhelming that the probability is that "know-how" and "common sense" would normally be used. In fact, a small period of work by an outside specialist to write a programme plus hired, inexpensive computer time provided management with a daily work schedule for the contract. An up-dated schedule was provided each week in the light of progress. These cases illustrate the way in which management is using new tools to solve problems better and faster than by hunch and past experience.

Another development of great importance is the practical possibility of building up in a business an integrated Management Information System. Earlier in this book, the importance of relevant, timely information for managers was stressed as the means by which effective control and decisions were made. The difficulties of providing this control information were also discussed.

For example:

— the complexity and volume of information required;
— the cost of producing it compared with the benefits;
— the unreliability of some data stemming particularly from difficulties in accurately capturing source data generated within the business;
— incomplete data, particularly that arising from the outside environment.

A recent paper by Bridgman and Green(55) points out that a Management Information System (M.I.S.) is analogous to a nervous system which will help management to sense inbalance and to control the business more efficiently—management will still be the brains! The distinguishing features of the M.I.S. of the future they see are:

"1. For the first time the specific need for, and existence of information systems is being recognised. The flow of information is being recognised as important to the efficient running of a company as is the flow of money, men and materials.

2. An M.I.S. will integrate the processes of:

   (a) Data gathering
   (b) Data storage
   (c) Data processing
   (d) Data transmission

3. This integration will add flexibility and strength to the business of management by:

   (a) Providing access to all information within a business relevant to a particular decision.
   (b) Reducing the importance of time and distance constraints.
   (c) Improving communication within a company so that it becomes a less restrictive factor in determining organisation.

10

4. Some technical facilities are now available for the first time because of advances in computing technology. Amongst these facilities are:

   (a) Unified records

   All records can be kept centrally in a data bank and are unique. No longer will different departments in an engineering business keep their own versions of parts lists, for instance.

   (b) One shot approach

   An item of data is entered into the system only once. All records affected by a particular item will be amended in a single sequence so that discrepancies resulting from amendments to records in different departments will disappear.

   (c) Automation

   All decisions that can be quantified and programmed in advance can be automated. Such decisions tend to be at the operating level of an enterprise rather than at a strategic level where the manager is concerned with unstructured broader policy decisions.

   (d) Information retrieval

   Falling costs of bulk storage make it increasingly possible to record information relevant to the company's business so that it can be retrieved on an ad hoc basis."

A by-product of such a Management Information System is that it makes possible—perhaps compels—radical changes in organisation, particularly in reducing the levels of management in the hierarchy as more routine decisions are taken away from the individual. Less drudgery leaves more time for the manager to use his unique characteristics of creativity, leadership and making decisions where the rules are imprecise. In the language of the Glacier Management project, the "prescribed" part of his work will go to the computer leaving the manager more time for the "discretionary" part. Moreover, our present traditional thinking about the divisions of functions and departments will be challenged, and there will be a new look at the centralisation/decentralisation pattern.

136

Top management must monitor developments in this total field with skill and interest. The implications for every aspect of "Improving Business Results"—determining objectives, identifying the optimum product/market mix, financial and non-financial controls, the selection and training of managers, organisation patterns—are very great indeed. Moreover, the speed of progress is accelerating: in the present decade the sum spent on information system equipment will multiply 4 or 5 times, whilst the actual performance of the equipment will also improve enormously. By 1973 the cost/performance ratio improvement may be in the order of seven to one.

To conclude: Improving Business Results is constantly being refined and developed. Already it is an approach which the Chief Executive can use with confidence in improving company profit and growth, and in creating the demanding business environment in which managers will grow.

PART SIX

THE
PRACTICAL
EXPERIENCE
OF
THREE
COMPANIES

KLM ROYAL DUTCH AIRLINES INTRODUCING A MANAGEMENT BY OBJECTIVES PROGRAMME INTO THE WORLDWIDE FIELD ORGANISATION

by

D. K. van HOUTEN

General Manager

KLM Royal Dutch Airlines
Schiphol Airport
AMSTERDAM

INTRODUCING A MANAGEMENT BY OBJECTIVES PROGRAMME INTO THE WORLDWIDE FIELD ORGANISATION

KLM Royal Dutch Airlines is one of the major international airline companies. Although half the capital is owned by the Dutch government the company operates on a strictly commercial basis, with its stock registered on the Amsterdam and New York Stock Exchanges. The financial bond with America is one indication of the company's close relationship with that country—for example the whole aircraft fleet is American made. The size and complexity of operations is indicated by a workforce of 13,900 people, about a third of them non-Dutch nationals, operating in some 70 countries with sales activities embracing more than 200 offices. The company's total annual revenue now exceeds 200 million U.S. dollars, of which 75% is derived from passage, 20% freight and 5% mail revenue. The annual growth rate has been in the order of 10% to 12%.

PRESSURES AND PROBLEMS

A major problem facing all airlines, including KLM, is the rising cost of operation combined with decreasing price and rates. For example, a return fare over the North Atlantic in 1946 was 644 dollars but the same journey now can be made for 265 dollars; this inevitably creates a pressure for constant improvement in business productivity. Moreover, in the last decade the market situation has changed from a buyer's to a seller's market. Another challenge to sales management in KLM is the extremely diverse range of markets in which the airline operates. These vary from, for example, the home market where the selling operation can be likened to a mass market operation in a sophisticated country, to other parts of the world where selling air transportation and freight can be understood best as the marketing of luxury goods. These diverse conditions demand an extremely flexible approach without losing a uniform KLM image.

Quite recently, KLM made a radical change in its organisation structure in order to increase effectiveness and flexibility, and to provide maximum possible delegation. Basically, this was a change from a functional to a geographical structure. The responsibility for the successful operating of KLM's business throughout the world is delegated to a field Organisation divided into a number of Areas, each with its Area Manager. These Areas consist of a group of countries, or Regions, each with its Establishment or Regional Manager. These Managers in turn control a series of District Managers. "Staff" support is given at the appropriate organisational level by specialists in such activities as passenger marketing, freight marketing, advertising, market research, personnel, and accountancy.

The combined influence of these problems and the new demands made on individual managers led top management to consider whether a management by objectives programme could further improve personal job performance and overall selling efficiency in the areas, country establishments and districts.

PRELIMINARY WORK

Two very important preliminary stages were necessary. The first was to make a thorough analysis of the real needs of the situation and this investigation was made by a joint team of KLM staff and outside management consultants. A wide cross section of people were interviewed at various levels and in a sample of countries, and many more contributed their ideas through a questionnaire. In this way a significant sample of managers in the Field Organisation were able to clarify the problems they faced and the areas in which they would welcome help. This, coupled with top management's own assessment, made clear the priorities. The importance of this thorough investigation is twofold. It gave much richer insight into needs than could otherwise have been obtained. Perhaps even more important it got operating managers positively involved right from the beginning so that they knew they had helped to shape subsequent action. The investigation led to the recommendation that a combined attack was required, using management by objectives on site in the Areas and Districts and supporting this with a series of central two week training courses.

The second of the preliminary stages was to undertake pilot work in two Areas and to run a prototype course. In this way the most appropriate techniques for KLM could be designed and their validity tested before there was any commitment to a full scale application.

141

THE PERFORMANCE IMPROVEMENT PROGRAMME

A critical review by top management of the pilot work led to the conclusion that KLM would derive worthwhile benefits from a planned extension throughout the whole field organisation. The typical steps in the programme can be summarised thus:

1. Performance Improvement in the Areas and Districts.

The starting point in any given Unit is for the senior manager to re-examine critically the basic objectives he is seeking to achieve; to look for new opportunities which should be pursued and to detail the difficulties and obstacles to securing better results. This analysis draws on the ideas of his subordinates and is discussed and finally agreed with his superior.

Every manager in the unit also makes an analysis of the key results he must achieve; the performance standards and criteria associated with them and the control data required to measure the marketing effectiveness of the performance generated. At the same time, the manager is encouraged to challenge every aspect of the job—its purpose, standards, controls and so on— KLM believe there is little point in merely defining more accurately what exists; the challenge is to change the present situation for something better. This draft analysis, called a "Job Results Guide", is then discussed and agreed with the manager's immediate boss.

From this emerges clear cut action plans, typically for the next six months, in which both manager and the boss commit themselves to improving results in areas which are defined as being of special importance to the unit.

In preparing these documents we have found the role of an independent Adviser or "catalyst" of vital importance—these are trained KLM men and outside consultants working jointly as a team. It is not their job to say what the "Job Results Guide" or "Action Plans" shall include, but their capacity to stimulate new thought and their ability to help managers to make an objective assessment of problems has proved to be influential in securing high quality results. As with the preliminary

142

investigation, the programme is concerned to involve managers very deeply in improving themselves on a continuous basis. An integral part of the programme is the review of performance at which the manager and his boss assess the way in which the Job Guide has been fulfilled and the agreed Action Plans implemented. This review leads to further Action Plans and is, of course, worthwhile evidence in developing training and career programmes.

2. Central Training Courses

Intensive two-week training courses are provided at which 16 managers from various parts of the world gain a deeper insight into the marketing policy of KLM; are instructed in various marketing and selling techniques and spend a good deal of time in understanding and practising techniques of Management by Objectives. Great stress is laid on participatory sessions, discussion groups, practical syndicate exercises and the pace of work is very high indeed. With a few exceptions the course leaders and speakers are either KLM staff or consultants who are involved in the field organisation work; this ensures a relevancy and acceptability of contribution. These courses have commanded the personal time and support of the most senior managers of KLM and this has been influential in making it clear that the training courses are an integral part of the basic job of managing the business better. Critical evaluation of content, speakers and other material ensures that the courses are under constant review. Apart from the knowledge and skills acquired in this short time—and the stimulus to study further the extensive reference notes which are issued—there are further but "hard to measure" benefits. A better sense of common purpose is created; attitudes become more constructive; those with practical exposure to the management by objectives programme discuss their experiences with men from countries where the programme has yet to be introduced. The establishment of a common frame of reference and terminology facilitates communications.

SOME GENERAL LESSONS

So far the management by objectives programme has been introduced into the Establishments of Italy, Switzerland, France,

Mexico, United Kingdom, Netherlands, Belgium, Lebanon, U.S.A. and Canada. Ten courses have been run at the Urwick Management Centre in the United Kingdom. Certain lessons seem to have general application.

— It is pointless to agree upon performance standards for individual managers until the unit objectives have been thoroughly re-examined and clarified. Otherwise there is a real danger of channelling new enthusiasm into unimportant areas or even of getting individuals "to do the wrong things better".

— It is dangerous and misconceived to hurry the process. The object of the programme is *not* just to produce a few pieces of paper. It is to get every manager to think through what is really important for him to achieve in the light of rapidly changing environmental and market factors. Attitudes cannot just be changed over-night and time, patience and persistent counselling may be necessary if a *lasting* benefit is to be obtained.

— The Adviser or 'catalyst" role is of great importance in helping managers to make this fresh appraisal of their objectives and their performance. It follows that the people assigned to the work, whether from inside or outside the business, must be of high quality and maturity and thoroughly trained in the latest techniques.

— The importance of the positive participation by line management has been repeatedly confirmed. This is not a programme which can have any lasting value if it is imposed on line managers. The programme must be shaped at every stage by line managers and it should be clear that their active support and personal involvement will not (and should not!) continue unless performance and profit results measurably improve.

RESULTS

The best testimony to the results so far achieved is top management's determination to extend the work throughout the field organisation worldwide. It is always difficult to isolate the impact of one change when many others are taking place at the same time: but it is striking that those countries where the programme is established are doing well in terms of sales and profitability. Managers in every country have identified areas for improvement, for example:

— rationalisation of local organisation;
— reduced overhead costs;
— better penetration into selected markets;
— more precise control information;
— new insight into customers' needs;

and have, through Action Plans, secured the improvements.

There is a unanimous opinion that individual managers are much clearer about what they have to achieve and this better sense of purpose is directed more accurately to meet the unit objectives.

A by-product of this clarity and the regular performance reviews associated with the programme has been a more perceptive view of the strengths and weaknesses of managers. Unexpected potential has been demonstrated and succession and training plans are more objective.

One very important result is a change in attitude amongst the Managers in the Field Organisation about the very nature of their job. Many of them regarded themselves essentially as high level salesmen, although they were responsible for teams of subordinates and often hundreds of thousands of dollars of marketing expenditure in complex market conditions. The recognition—and supporting action to go with it—by such men that they are primarily *managers* is one key factor in the improved business results which are now being secured.

CONCLUSION

It will be clear from this brief case history that management by objectives is a sharp cutting tool which requires courage and determination to use to good effect. It exposes vividly what can be improved, and these improvements can be made at higher as well as at lower management levels. No top management should use it unless they are ready to find out these 'home truths' and are prepared to put in high quality support and follow through to secure improvement. But, given top management support, it can generate that sense of purpose and receptivity to change on which continued profitability depends. KLM regard this programme as one of a number of dynamic ways in which it seeks to improve its effectiveness, and thus to serve the public better.

LAPORTE INDUSTRIES LTD.
IMPROVING BUSINESS RESULTS AT
FULLERS EARTH UNION LTD.

by

W. WOODHALL

Deputy Managing Director
Laporte Industries Ltd.

IMPROVING BUSINESS RESULTS AT FULLERS' EARTH UNION LIMITED

FULLERS' EARTH UNION LIMITED is a subsidiary company of Laporte Industries Limited—a substantial British chemical group. It mines or quarries its raw materials close to its works, and subjects the material to a number of physical and chemical processes to produce a range of products, mainly for industrial use. The number of employees was about 700 and the capital employed some £ 2 million. Today, with a significantly increased output, the capital employed is approximately the same and the number of employees is now 590.

The Company faced a serious situation in 1963. The demand for its products had been adversely affected by changes in the technology of important customers. Moreover, an important nd sophisticated new chemical plant was proving difficult to get on stream, and overhead and production costs were mounting severely. At that time there seemed little prospect of a return to the level of profitability which the Company had earned for the Group consistently in the past.

With the guidance of consultants we decided to deal with the situation in three ways:

1. To take such action as we could to make short-term improvements in profitability.
2. To initiate studies leading to a strategic forward plan with supporting tactical plans—thus rethinking the future policy of the Company.
3. To introduce the concepts of Management by Objectives, in order to help individual managers to re-think and clarify their new priorities in a changed situation.

A. SHORT-TERM IMPROVEMENTS

By the time these decisions were being implemented the Company's position had deteriorated further and a small loss was being forecasted for the current year.

Immediate action was taken to reduce production, mining and transport overhead costs, including changes in the organisation

148

and better methods of planning and control. More savings were achieved through reducing unnecessary plant maintenance, direct labour and general administrative costs. It was possible to make important changes in the product range so that, for example, 64 main grades of high quality product were reduced to 24.

These short-term improvements, worth about £ 100,000 per annum, were achieved between March and September, 1963.

B. STRATEGIC AND TACTICAL PLANNING

Simultaneously with these short-term improvements, the Company assessed the external environment. Economic and political factors in major markets were analysed, together with likely trends in technological developments in these markets. In the main this work was carried out by our own management team, though guided in principle by the consultants and assisted by some specialist advice. The results of the early studies led to a series of papers on:

— present and future uses of current products, and the strengths and weaknesses of competing materials and processes;
— the Company's performance in terms of product/market mix;
— assessment of the financial and marketing positions of all main competitors and potential competitors, world-wide;
— profitability in various markets and pricing policies relative to competitors;
— assessment of sources, qualities and economics of major raw materials;

and later on further analyses of:

— the Company's cost structure and possibilities for cost reduction;
— assessment of the output, quality, profitability and future objectives of the new chemical plant which was causing trouble;
— assessment of the condition, utility and life of all manufacturing plant from the viewpoint of cost, quality, maintenance and profit.

The completion and interpretation of these studies took some six months. They enabled us to focus attention on the salient features of the situation, which were:

1. Profitability of the various grades of products varied substantially.
2. Profitability was highest on those grades whose markets were being lost.
3. Profitability of much export business was marginal.
4. We were over-rating the strength of foreign competition in export markets.
5. There were good growth prospects for our products, but mainly in grades currently earning low gross margins.
6. New markets were available to us.
7. Overhead costs had increased at a faster rate than the Company's growth, and there was scope for reducing them.

Most of these facets of the business had been known to top management before these studies, but now we were examining them in depth and looking at them as a total problem.

At this stage we at Group set out clearly the minimum requirements for any strategic Plan adopted by the Fullers' Earth Union Limited. These included:

1. The achievement of a minimum profit before tax within two years—and this minimum was stated.
2. The achievement of profits before tax of at least 15% per annum on the capital employed continuously thereafter, for each major section of the business.
3. The establishment of detailed plans for growth and expansion.

The Company had, by February 1964, set out detailed and quantified plans for the next five years, forecasting a substantial rise in return on capital from 1964/65 to 1968/69.

Some of the features of this Strategic Plan were:

— to arrive at a price structure designed to discourage other producers from entering the world's markets and, through efficiency and cost reduction, to ensure that product prices

150

in markets outside the U.S.A. were maintained below levels which would interest American producers;

— increase sales volume, mainly in selected overseas markets for high grade products and in home markets for low grade products;

— expand top quality high grade home sales by introducing new grades which would under-cut imports from overseas. This in turn required changes in the new chemical plant.

— further reduce overhead expenditure;

— reduce production and process direct costs;

— a re-assessment of the capital expenditure programme. Mistaken thinking had led to severe cuts in the capital expenditure programme, since it was wrongly thought that the Company could not afford anything else. This re-assessment led to increased expenditure on cost-reducing modernisation and some retrenchment where unprofitable markets were being chased;

— direct research expenditure to projects where potential profits had been identified.

The Strategic Plan was then converted into a series of detailed Tactical Plans for each part of the Company.

C. IMPROVING MANAGEMENT PERFORMANCE

To convert these objectives into true elements of personal accountability, every manager developed an analysis of his key tasks with performance standards and controls. In addition, each manager had an action plan setting out clearly the improvements he was responsible for achieving in a set period. A trained counsellor or adviser assisted managers in this analysis.

Whilst control and review of results was a normal part of daily management, the discipline of having a formal three-month review of progress with each man was instituted. The manager had a frank discussion with his boss and a revised set of expected results was established for the next period. This review also included an assessment of the man's suitability for the job he was holding, his potential for different work and his training needs. The whole process of setting and agreeing objectives and

151

discussing results was vital in getting Company plans implemented with enthusiasm and commitment. Fullers' Earth Union Limited is acutely aware that profit is achieved not by plans alone, but by plans put into action by good managers.

An important feature of Improving Business Results through profit planning and better manager performance is the need for tight control by the Chief Executive. The company up-dates its Plan quarterly so that there is always a year's view ahead, of which the next period is broken down into one-monthly accounting units. The quarterly review is taken very seriously indeed, since it gives everyone a rigorous discipline to re-examine not only their results but their forward improvement plans.

The Company faces many continuing difficulties at a time of economic uncertainty in Britain and the accelerating pace of change in technology and market conditions. So far, however, the results of this work are bearing fruit, and some examples of this include:

— the Group Chairman stated in his report for the year 1964/65. "It might mislead to express the year's profit—for the Fullers' Earth Union Limited—as a percentage increase on that of the previous year, as the figure would be so high. Last year the profit was at an abnormally low level and a major re-organisation and modernisation was planned. This process is now proceeding, and already the result has been a really striking improvement in profits, which are now running at a very satisfactory level."

This progress continues.

— morale, sense of purpose and confidence throughout the management group is vastly higher. Decisions are taken more effectively at lower levels;

— forward planning is slowly growing into a way of life, an attitude of mind, rather than a "new technique";

— the link between company and individual objectives is improving and reviews provide a valuable feedback of difficulties;

152

— there is less parochialism and departmentalism in thinking. Most people recognise the inter-dependence of functions and units when the acid test applied by top management is "What impact will this have on profit?";
— the Company is expecting some further loss of business through technological change, but they are now anticipating this and successfully making alternative plans to fill the gap.

The Company intends to maintain this progress in future by using the most effective management methods available.

The story of this Company is well illustrated by the profit record over the period concerned. If the profits achieved in 1960/61 are taken as 100, then results are:

$$
\begin{array}{ll}
1960/61 & - \ 100 \\
1961/62 & - \ \ 64 \\
1962/63 & - \ \ 38 \\
1963/64 & - \ \ 18 \\
1964/65 & - \ 100 \\
1965/66 & - \ 135 \\
1968/69 & - \ 160 \ \text{(Projected)}
\end{array}
$$

Finally, not the least important lesson learned in this exercise was that the ability to analyse the facts of the case and to plan change, and the ability to implement the plan was present in the management team. Crystallising all this into the successful results achieved was largely due to the guidance given by the consultants and to the eventual adoption at all levels of clearly defined objectives.

MANAGEMENT BY OBJECTIVES IN SMITHS INDUSTRIES LTD.

by

M. W. B. KNIGHT

Special Director
Smiths Industries Ltd.

MANAGEMENT BY OBJECTIVES IN SMITHS INDUSTRIES LTD.

SMITHS INDUSTRIES LIMITED (SI) employ about 24,000 people in the United Kingdom in light engineering and electronics. The Company is organised in a number of Divisions which manufacture and market a wide range of instruments and accessories for the automobile and aviation industries, aviation and marine control systems, radar and electronic equipment, industrial instrumentation, clocks and watches and a number of other products.

In 1964 the main Board set up a small central management development advisory service under a Management Development Adviser (MDA) who reports directly to the Chairman and Managing Director. The MDA has two inter-related tasks: to formalise and extend the Company's procedures for 'traditional' management development (i.e. management manpower planning, recruitment, appraisal systems, education and training, policy regarding the filling of vacancies, and so on); and to develop and progressively introduce a system for improving management performance by the setting of objectives at unit and individual manager levels.

This paper is concerned mainly with the setting of objectives, and describes how a scheme that was at first concerned with improving individual manager performance by target setting, has evolved into an instrument which management can use also to improve the performance of whole units and formations of units.

However, since management by objectives will reach its full effectiveness only when it is applied from Board level downwards, we first give our view of the system as a whole.

THE SYSTEM AS A WHOLE.

An objective is a definition of where a business—its Board, its formations, its units or even its individual managers—wants to go. It has three essential elements: it must define the starting point or present position, it must specify the finishing point, and it must state the time by which the goal is to be reached. And

156

the end result must be quantitative, or at least positively identifiable. To give a common example: "To increase profitability on assets employed" is often said to be the objective of a Board. To us it is no more than a pious hope. "To increase profitability from $x\%$ on £ Am. assets employed to $y\%$ on £ Bm. assets employed, by August 1969" *is* an objective. Disciplined research and planning must have been undertaken before it could be defined and—if it is to be achieved—a great deal of subsequent planning and co-ordinated action will be needed at all levels in the enterprise. The business will be forced to review its markets and products—and perhaps look for new ones— and to examine with critical eyes its marketing and selling functions, its production facilities and techniques, and so on; and subsidiary objectives will in fact have to be set in all these areas if the overall aim is to be met. A start will, in effect, have been made on formal long range planning. This, in an ideal world, is the best possible way to introduce management by objectives. Nevertheless the system *can* be applied with success to units even in the absence of overall profit plans.

Objectives, whether generated from on high or from within a unit, are by themselves not enough. In our experience the mere setting of them rarely achieves the goal. Every objective must be broken down into defined action to be taken by named units and managers by specified times. And the action itself must be carefully monitored and controlled to produce the predicted, measurable results that will directly contribute to the attainment of the objective concerned.

It is with this work at unit level, the work of helping individual managers to specify the results they mean to achieve, of helping Units to define and achieve specific objectives for improvement, that we have so far had most of our experience and which we now describe.

THE SYSTEM AT UNIT LEVEL.

The system can be summarised as follows:

(a) Each manager in a unit from foreman, supervisor, or area sales manager up to and including the unit manager, analyses his *own* job with the active help of a Management Analyst (MA).

(b) **This** analysis is not a job description of the usual sort. It specifies not only the main areas of responsibility of the jobholder (the Key Result Areas or KRAs), but also the actual results to be achieved and targets to be hit, and the means by which progress can be measured and controlled. And it contains specific suggestions for improvements wherever these appear to be possible.

(c) Each manager and his superior then get together—again with an MA in attendance—to discuss, amend and finally agree on the job analysis, and to decide upon the action to be taken to improve performance. They produce together a written individual job improvement plan which both undertake to follow.

(d) At regular intervals thereafter—every 3 to 6 months depending upon the level of the job—the manager meets formally with his superior to review the results and improvements being achieved, and to formulate a new improvement plan for the next period.

(e) As the individual job analyses go on, the head of the Unit is helped to formulate an overall Unit Improvement Plan which sets out the objectives to be achieved by the Unit, breaks these down into timed action by individuals, and sets up a strong system of control.

THE INDIVIDUAL JOB ANALYSIS.

Some extracts from individual job analyses, which we call a MANAGEMENT GUIDE are shown in Exhibit 15. The Management Guide is essentially the same as the Key Results Analysis described in the main text of this book.

It is by no means as easy as it looks to analyse a job in these terms. We have found that initially most managers need a great deal of help in thinking through their job in this new way; they in fact usually require four or five half-day sessions with the MA, spread over several weeks to allow for careful thought and analysis between sessions, before their minds are adjusted to thinking in terms of specific results and controls.

THE INDIVIDUAL JOB IMPROVEMENT PLAN.

When the Management Guide is in final draft form, it is discussed by the manager and his superior, with the MA present. This usually results in a good deal of redrafting— but at the end of it, after two or three hours of hard work, they are agreed upon the KRAs and key tasks, the carefully defined results and targets to be achieved, and the control information by which they will both judge progress; and they have discussed and analysed the manager's suggestions for improved performance.

The scale and range of individual managers' suggestions have surprised us. A dozen actionable ideas from one manager is not abnormal—rarely is the score less than four. In one Unit employing 600 people a hundred individual suggestions have been adopted and the Unit as a whole has set itself twenty-seven money-making objectives for improvement in efficiency. These suggestions range from minor administrative and technical improvements to quite major innovations and changes in organisation. It is no wonder, therefore, that the superior manager pays careful attention to the suggestions column when he reviews his subordinate's Management Guide. Each of the suggestions is marked with a letter I, S, or M. Those marked 'I' are for the individual action of the manager himself and a number of them (usually not more than 2 or 3 at a time) will be agreed as targets to be hit during the immediate future. Those marked 'S' are for supporting action by the immediate superior manager. Those marked 'M' will be collected together from this and other Management Guides by the MA, who will analyse them and refer them to the overall unit manager for consideration, and possibly for inclusion in the Unit Improvement Plan.

It remains for the manager and his superior to discuss the priorities within the job specified in the Management Guide. The manager will of course try to hit all his targets. But at any given time there are likely to be some which top management considers to be of vital importance. Note will therefore be taken of the key result areas, tasks and targets which require priority attention during the coming period.

The manager will leave the interview with his superior with an approved Management Guide, and with a personal "Job

Improvement Plan" which will clearly lay down the specific improvements he has undertaken to achieve. Recorded also will be the action his superior has agreed to take, and the training he has agreed to provide, in his support—an important and highly motivating consideration.

An example of a "Job Improvement Plan" is shown as Exhibit 16.

JOB REVIEW.

The Manager will now go into action and will expect, and should of course receive, day-to-day and week-to-week encouragement and support from his superior. But, in addition, at the end of the agreed period of say 3—6 months the two of them will meet to review the job formally—the *job,* it should be noted, and not the manager who is doing it. This review meeting will normally occupy the best part of a morning or an afternoon. All concerned will have studied the control information specified in the Management Guide, and will have compared predicted results with actual achievements, before the meeting takes place.

At the meeting each predicted result and each target in the Management Guide will be discussed in turn in relation to its control information, and the simple question asked: "has it or has it not been achieved?". If it has been achieved, the question will be asked: "should it remain for the next period, or could an improved target be set?"—and the Management Guide will thus be brought up-to-date. If it has not been achieved, there will be neither recrimination nor blame. The question will simply be asked: "what action can *we* take to see that it is achieved during the next period?". From this an action plan will emerge, which can conveniently be combined with the next Job Improvement Plan. It will:

(i)   list results and targets not being achieved but still considered desirable and achievable and, opposite each;

(ii) state what action the superior manager will take to assist his subordinate in achieving the target;

(iii) define the action the individual manager will take to ensure that he achieves the target;

160

(iv) and, finally, list any training that will be provided to the manager or to his subordinates in order to facilitate achievement of each specific result or target concerned.

The job review meeting will then consider the individual improvements the manager undertook to achieve during the period under review, will check results, and will decide what further action is required.

Finally, the revised Management Guide will be approved and a new Job Improvement Plan will be set for the next period.

This cycle of events will then repeat itself and will become, in effect, an installed system of management of individual roles within the unit.

Job reviews are vital. In our experience it is the first of these that really brings the Management Guide to life. It is essential that the MA should be present at the first two or three reviews that any manager conducts: intermediate and even senior managers need help and practice before they can review a job in such a way as to get the maximum benefit, the maximum action, from it. We have found that many prescribed results are not achieved, many targets are not hit, during the first period after a Management Guide is completed, sometimes because the job-holder has been 'too busy doing other things' (in one case a senior foreman, for example, had been too busy progress chasing, going to the engineers for drawings, and so on, to hit his important targets. When this became apparent positive action was taken by the factory's top management to remedy the situation both for him and for others): and often, regrettably, targets are missed because the manager's superior has for one reason or another been unable to complete the supporting action that he had undertaken. We have found that the occasional attendance of the unit manager at review sessions, on a random basis, is a great help and usually leads to positive action by all concerned during the ensuing period.

THE UNIT IMPROVEMENT PLAN.

The plans of senior formations, the views of senior management, the suggestions of managers in their Management Guides and

161

the contributions of MAs and other specialists, all combine to provide the raw material for a total Unit Improvement Plan.

As in individual Management Guides our analysis of the objectives to be achieved by the Unit as a whole can conveniently be conducted under a number of headings or KRAs: 'Productivity and Production Efficiency', 'Factory Costs & Profitability', 'Control of Production', 'Product Quality', 'Recruitment, Training & Development', 'Introduction of New Products, Processes & Plant', are typical in a factory. Under each heading we define the factors in the present situation that give rise to the possibility of action to effect a really significant gain in efficiency or reduction in cost. Against each of these we then delve, measure, and finally reason out the objectives— the goals that must be reached to achieve a satisfying improvement in performance.

We carefully define these objectives (illustration at Exhibit 17), break each down into the action to be taken by named managers, and bar-chart the timing of each element in the plan (Exhibits 17/18). These documents are held in a looseleaf booklet which becomes the Unit's 'master' Improvement Plan. A carefully contrived review mechanism is also installed to ensure that the Head of the Unit can monitor and control the progress of the teams of managers working on the various objectives. We have this system working in a number of units now: it is certainly a very powerful method for stimulating purposeful action, which after all is what management by objectives is all about.

INSTALLING THE SYSTEM.

Before the system is installed in any unit the Managing Director of the Company or Division must be fully behind the venture, as must also the functional director in charge and the head of the unit itself.

The first thing to do on entering a unit is to brief the unit manager and agree with him which of his subordinate managers will be involved in the exercise. We next brief ourselves thoroughly on the key objectives and key result areas likely to apply in the

162

particular unit and thought to be important by its top management. This is achieved in a series of 3 or 4 meetings with the head of the unit, and one or two of his senior staff if he wishes to invite them. A list of typical key areas for the type of unit concerned (example at Exhibit 19) is useful in provoking discussion of the unit's work. The sort of questions asked of the unit manager concerning each of the main headings in turn can be illustrated by taking 'Operator Performance' as an example:

'What are the main problems associated with operator performance? Where is performance less than satisfactory?'

'How is performance measured? What control documents are available?'

'Have you any specific objectives—i.e., plans for improvements in operator performance? What are they?'

'Which of your subordinates do you consider has primary responsibility for operator performance? i.e., who initiates action to improve performance?'

'What other managers contribute? How is their work co-ordinated and controlled?'

These talks with the head of the unit take place over 3 or 4 weeks, and during this time the MAs are busy familiarising themselves with the work of the unit. In a factory they will be working with foremen, superintendents and with the accountant, looking primarily at control information, searching for the measurements they know they will need in helping managers to specify results, to set their targets. This is a vital phase of our work. We must get to know the realities of what goes on—the real strengths and weaknesses—if we are to avoid superficiality.

We are now ready to start work with individual managers in the unit—as a matter of fact this individual work will probably already have been started at the lower levels during our period of 'reconnaissance'.

How do we decide in what order to tackle the functions within the unit? It is not good practice to produce Management Guides for random individuals: one must work through a unit as a whole, and within that unit through sections, departments, etc. The knowledge of the work actually being done, of targets

163

actually set, grows in this way so that by the time the MAs start their analysis with the higher levels of management they have a real understanding of the unit's problems which will help them in their catalytic function. We have also discovered that at the levels of management to be found in a typical works it is better to start producing individual Management Guides at the bottom (e.g. senior foreman level) rather than at the top (e.g. with the works manager). As a result of the analysis of jobs at the lower levels, functions are often altered, levels of responsibility and authority are changed and considerable reorganisation is effected. It is not until the real work has been studied at the lower levels that the help and support required by junior and middle management can be diagnosed and written into the jobs of their seniors. Our work has also confirmed the obvious: that in any type of unit it is essential to start with the line function, i.e. with production in a manufacturing unit, probably with production control coming a very close second. The other functions such as production engineering, work study, purchasing, personnel, especially accountancy, are servants of production—or they should be. Their targets cannot be set until the requirements of production are known.

We begin our individual work in a factory, then, with senior production foremen, followed by the production superintendents; we then spread out into production control and the other services, the senior production manager if there is one, and finally the works manager himself whose Management Guide is, of course, discussed and finalised between him and his Director, with the Group or Divisional MDA present. The same principle should apply to individual job analysis in other units—e.g. in a Sales unit the salesmen and area managers should come first, before top sales or marketing management is tackled.

As the production of individual Management Guides builds up, the Unit Improvement Plan begins to develop. There will be careful co-ordination between the requirements of the unit plan and the results being specified by individuals in their Guides: no clashes must occur, nor must there be division of effort.

Finally, then, the system is installed. Each manager has in his Management Guide his own checklist of the results he expects to achieve in his current job, and his individual Improvement

164

Plan. He also knows precisely his part in the overall Unit Improvement Plan. His work and the improvements he is effecting are being reviewed regularly with his superior, and action taken by both to remedy 'drift'. And the head of unit has organised teams, each with a co-ordinator, working on the unit's projects for improvement. The Director in charge of the whole function can also now monitor the performance of the head of unit at regular intervals through review of his personal Management Guide, and can direct and control the progress of the unit as a whole by review of the master Improvement Plan.

There remains the question of maintaining the system once it is installed. It will only be maintained if the head of the unit is enthusiastic about it, is determined to *use* it as a primary mechanism of control, and sets up a simple procedure to ensure that it rolls on and is kept up-to-date. He may need a high-calibre assistant to administer the procedure; and he should have the advice and occasional services of the MDA and a qualified MA when he needs their help.

TEAM STUDIES OF SPECIAL PROBLEMS.

Where a particular problem requires the attention of a number of managers, the head of the unit may decide to form a team to tackle it.

As always, the vital thing is that the reasoning processes used by the team should be carefully structured and that thought should be concentrated not on the problem itself, i.e. upon the difficulties, but on its effects on *results*—i.e. upon opportunities for improvement. Thus, as in a Management Guide, we start by isolating the KRAs of the unit or business which are adversely affected by the problem. Against each of these KRAs the team defines the specific results which, if achieved, will indicate satisfactory performance. We list these under the heading 'WHAT WE WANT'. The brainstorming session then turns its attention to 'WHAT PREVENTS US'—i.e. the obstacles that are now preventing achievement of each of the desirable results specified under the previous heading. Finally an analysis of the obstacles to achievement leads to a specific plan of action by *management* to remove them, listing the action required, who is to take it, by when it is to be completed. This may of course be incorporated in the Unit Improvement Plan.

12

Identifying 'what we want' (the results that would satisfy us if they could be achieved) and 'what prevents us' (the obstacles to be removed by management) is not difficult once the real result areas that are affected by the problem have been clearly established. It is worth saying again that the key to the whole process is to avoid being mesmerised by the problem itself, and to focus attention instead on isolating the key results—the business objectives—that are being adversely affected by it. An example may help:

(a) 'Industrial Relations' (which is certainly not in itself a business objective) was found to be a major problem and the Works Manager formed a small team to study it.

(b) After a lot of discussion the team had still not even decided what they meant by industrial relations, which is a notably woolly area in most people's minds. Attention was therefore focused upon the result areas that were being adversely affected by industrial relations. Among them, for example, were:

— Ability to achieve the programme (affected by restrictive practices of various sorts).
— Ability to introduce new machinery (operator resistance was causing long delays).
— Ability to introduce new methods (long delays again).
— Ability to improve operator performance (refusal to accept re-study, etc.)

and so on—once the team started to think in this way the main areas were easily identified.

(c) The process of analysis then proceeded and, somewhat to our surprise, the long lists of 'obstacles'—the self-diagnosed reasons for inadequate performance in the field of industrial relations—were in the end seen to condense themselves into quite a small number of areas for management action: e.g.

(i) the need for overhaul and rationalisation of the wages structure and incentive schemes (quite clear criteria emerged from the study);
(ii) the need for rationalisation of work standards in certain areas;

(iii) the need for clarification of policy concerning for example conditions of service, job security, redundancy terms, sharing the fruits of increased productivity, and so on;

(iv) the need for improved operator training, and for management training in defined fields.

As a result of this study, objectives were defined and agreed by the Works Manager with his Production Director, and action is now going ahead. An overhaul of the wages system has been effected, the work study department has been reorganised, managers and senior shop stewards have been trained in Primary Standard Data (a synthetic system of work measurement) and this is being applied; and training of operators has been intensified.

The team study procedure takes time, but has the advantage of motivation: managers who have taken part have thought through their own problems and found ways of solving them. Very positive action has resulted from the studies we have so far undertaken.

THE PAY-OFF.

The really big pay-off from the introduction of management by objectives in a unit undoubtedly lies in the increased individual efficiency and enthusiasm of the managers themselves. People who *use* the system really do become better and more effective managers. Already we have evidence of a noticeable change in the attitude of managers who have thought through their jobs in terms of the results they are to achieve, and of whom it is required—indeed who require of themselves—that they should achieve specific improvements within specified periods of time. In particular an excellent team spirit is engendered among those who play a part in the Unit Improvement Plan. But there are other benefits to be gained. Here are a few examples of the many changes that have occurred as a result of our work:

(a) Analysis of the jobs of a number of line and service managers in a factory revealed overlapping. As a result of this, and of the team study on industrial relations referred to above, the Works Manager reorganised his two separate production

167

units into a single unit under one manager, and regrouped a number of the service functions under a productivity manager—with significant increases in efficiency and without requiring additional personnel.

(b) The writing of Management Guides for two senior inspectors in one unit led to the appointment of an overall quality manager and the introduction of the concept of total quality control from design engineering right through production, without additional personnel. The quality manager is now driving ahead to achieve the specific targets laid down in his Management Guide.

(c) A series of suggestions from several managers led to the inclusion in another unit's improvement plan of an objective to reduce excess manufacturing costs by £ 400 per week: they now form the team that is well on the way to achieving this result.

(d) In the same unit, managers' suggestions have been so prolific that action has had to be carefully 'rationed' to accord with priorities. Already completed are, for example, a top to bottom revision of quality standards, the introduction of statistical quality control and preventive inspection (40% reduction of inspection staff in some sections), retraining of setters and reorganisation of their duties, the setting of stringent targets for machine utilisation and efficiency and the introduction of machine loading procedures (work no longer has to be sub-contracted), the installation of methods improvements by teams of supervisors and work people (40 job improvements in one department alone), and so on. The list is endless.

(e) In three factories the unit accountants have undertaken a complete review of the flow of control information to meet the needs revealed by Management Guides.

(f) The Management Guides of two senior sales managers showed that they lacked marketing support—e.g. in market and customer research, statistical forecasting, product and packaging design and styling, etc. The marketing function is now being overhauled under a new Marketing Director.

168

(g) In a Marketing and Sales Department, attempts to set targets for gross and net profit margins for individual products led to an analysis of real (as opposed to allocated) product costs. The results were most revealing, and have led to the repricing of many products and to plans to replace others with more profitable lines.

CONCLUSION.

Our experience at Unit level has amply demonstrated that the system of Management by Objectives is a very powerful tool indeed in the hands of progressive managers, and it is our hope that it will become the standard practice of management in Smiths Industries. No-one who is willing to devote resources to it need hesitate for fear that it will not pay ample dividends.

EXHIBIT 15

KEY RESULT AREAS/TASKS	CURRENT PERFORMANCE TARGETS

EXAMPLE I: ONE KRA FROM A ▮

CUSTOMER SERVICE.

To arrange and control call frequencies for all customers.

a) 'X' calls per cycle made on category 'A' customers.

'Y' calls per cycle on category 'B' customers.

'Z' calls per quarter on special accounts.

To establish with each customer the stock levels he should hold so that delivery times can be kept economic with minimum risk of stock-out.

b) Following delivery times are acceptable to customers and me▮

	90% Orders Within	97% Orders Within
Cat. 'A'	7 days	14 days
Cat. 'B'	4 days	7 days
Sp. Accts.	7 days	14 days

To ensure that products are displayed advantageously by customers and that point-of-sale aids are available to support promotions.

c) (i) Approved display aids are distributed and used as follow▮

Category 'A' customers - 7 point-of-sale aids per.............

Category 'B' customers - 5 point-of-sale aids per.............

(ii) At least X% of Cat. 'A' customers are mounting the displ▮ to each promotion plan.

(Other KRAs in this Guide include 'Achievement of Sales Targets', 'Developmen▮ Feedback of Market Information', 'Sales Forecasts and Budgets'.)

EXAMPLE II: ONE KRA FROM A G▮

INTRODUCTION OF NEW PRODUCTS AND ELIMINATION OF UNPROFITABLE LINES.

Key Tasks:

To control the gross margins on new products at above the level required in the Divisional profit plan.

To ensure within 5 years that no products remain in the range because of their contribution to overhead recovery rather than to profitability.

To achieve an economic compromise between production costs and production flexibility (i.e. the ability to meet the market needs for style changes, customer modifications to standard products, small batch orders for special products etc.).

a) No new product or model is put into production which ▮ lower gross margin on sales price than:

	Home
Mechanical '———	30%
Electrical '———	35%
Contract Work (own design)	25%
Contract Wk. (customer design)	20%

b) The overall percentage by value of products which achieve▮ the above target gross margins is reduced successively eac▮ 20% of present figure.

c) The size of orders undertaken by production which involve er▮ or production engineering work are not less than:

(i) Minor modifications to suit individual customer requir▮ not less than £10,000.

(ii) Special new products to individual customer's speci▮ initial order not less than £50,000.

(iii) New model to be added to our catalogue - estimate▮ sales value not less than £100,000.

d) The scheduled dates for the introduction of new products ▮ are not exceeded by more than one month.

e) All new products are systematically value engineered pric▮ introduction into production.

(Other KRAs in this Guide include Profitability and Profit Planning , Determin▮ and Human Relations'.)

EXTRACTS FROM TWO MANAGEMENT GUIDES

METHOD OF CHECKING PERFORMANCE	SUGGESTIONS FOR PERFORMANCE IMPROVEMENT	AGREED ACTION on SUGGESTIONS
MANAGER'S MANAGEMENT GUIDE		
men's reports.		
ey plans and logs.		
anding Orders Analysis.	If we are to meet even these generous delivery times reliably, either depot stocks of some items will have to be increased or lead times from the factory reduced. I suggest an OR investigation of optimum stock levels.	
mers complaints.		
rd of distribution of sales aids.	I suggest the sales training department should include in their sales reps' courses more instruction on how to persuade customers to use modern displays.	
orts from merchandising ager.		
smen's reports.		
onal Observation.		
s', 'Planning of Salesmen's Activities', 'Training, Directing and Motivating Salesmen',		
ER'S MANAGEMENT GUIDE		
roduct Review.	If we are to produce new models in the future which are going to command sales prices which provide adequate gross margins, I suggest that we shall have to strengthen our engineering—and especially our styling—facilities, even with some temporary inroads into profits..............	
roduct Review.	I suggest we need to set up some more definite annual procedure for evaluating the contribution made by each of our products, and for replacements to be programmed in good time.	
on Phase	We must dissuade Sales from regarding our factories as jobbing shops and get them thinking in terms of high volume production.	
ts (New Products).		
iation Documents.		
d New Product Schedules.	I intend to introduce a new system for shepherding new products through all their stages by Jan. 67, using Critical Path Analysis.	
orts.	At present our VA and VE have 'drifted' into little more than the collecting of good ideas from the various branches. I am introducing formal procedures and mean to see that they are followed.	
tation of Divisional Policies , Organisation Structure , Development of Management		

EXHIBIT 16

	Name	Position	Superior	Period covered by the Plan	Actual date of Review
JOB IMPROVEMENT PLAN		ASSEMBLY SUPERINTENDENT		FROM JUNE 1966 MID OCTOBER 1966	

Purpose of the document: It records the decisions taken at a Job Review meeting for action to improve job results.

NOTE—Non-achievement of agreed action will be regarded as a serious shortfall in performance unless the circumstances preventing achievement have been made known to the superior and recorded on the document during the period covered by the plan.

CONTRIBUTION TO UNIT IMPROVEMENT PLAN

i.e. Reference numbers of the action breakdown against Unit Objectives which directly involve the job holder.

17a, 17b, 20e, 21c, 24f

Comments by Superior on action taken:

Statement of the Problem or the need for action	Statement of the end-results aimed for in the period covered by the Plan	Step by step breakdown of the action required to achieve the end-results.	By Whom	Notes of circumstances preventing achievement (delays, amendments, etc.)	Superior's comments on action taken
1. It is still virtually impossible to plan assembly production more than 1 set ahead. Most of the foreman's and chargehand's time is taken up in progress chasing work. A better system for planning work is therefore desirable	1. Assembly programmes to exist one week ahead for each assembly section. 2. The percentage achievement of each programme to be not less than 90%.	1. To organise and preside over a weekly assembly progress meeting. 2. To attend weekly assembly progress meeting together with P.C., Buyer etc.	Production Manager. Job Holder		

	5. To keep a record of the number of times the agreed weekly programme is changed because of: (a) Shortages under the control of Buyer, P.C., etc. (b) Shortage of Labour. (c) Manufacturing Difficulties. (d) Other Reasons.	Job Holder		
	6. To review records weekly and to take action to improve performance.	Production Manager.		
2. The introduction of New Products is not sufficiently prepared in advance to avoid crises occurring at early stages of production.	1. Formal Planning Procedure for the introduction of New Products to be available.	1. To obtain the production target dates and rates for the clock.	Production Manager.	
	2. Planning Procedure to enable New Products to be introduced within ± 5 days of agreed production launch date and at the agreed production rates.	2. To establish the plan for the introduction of the clock in terms of labour requirements, tools, training etc.	Job Holder	
		3. To plan the build-up of production.	Job Holder	
		4. To review plan at weekly intervals until clock is in production.	Production Manager.	
		5. To evaluate the success of the plan and to make recommendations for improvements in planning.	Job Holder	

EXHIBIT 1

FACTORY IMPROVEMENT PLAN FOR 1966/67

THE KEY IMPROVEMENT AREAS

THE PROBLEMS WE HAVE TO SOLVE

OUR OBJECTIVES FOR THE CURRENT YEAR
(Completion date 31st August, 1967)

I. PRODUCTIVITY & PRODUCTION EFFICIENCY

1. Inconsistencies in the level of bonus earnings arising from varying degrees of loose time standards which give rise to dissatisfaction with earnings, poor labour flexibility and high labour turnover.

2. There are numerous jobs for which standard times have been established for many years and have been the subject of method changes without re-evaluation. Work specifications are out of date or in excess of the measured work content of the job. There is, therefore, no accurate yardstick for measuring operator effort.

3. The effectiveness of indirect labour performance is largely an unknown quantity which gives rise to doubts about their level of productivity.

4. There is very little factual knowledge of the effectiveness with which machines are utilised giving rise to the suspicion of operating inefficiency and their excessive overhead costs.

5. Our existing products are not being subjected to any form of systematic and critical reappraisal of design to facilitate improved production methods and reduced material costs.

1. TO HAVE RESTUDIED THE METHODS OF ALL JOBS IN
   FLEX MANUFACTURE
   FLEX ASSEMBLY
   PLASTIC
   AND TO HAVE ACHIEVED NOT LESS THAN 6% REDUCTION IN THE STANDARD LABOUR CONTENT.

2. TO HAVE RESTUDIED THE TIME STANDARDS FOR ALL JOBS IN
   FLEX MANUFACTURE
   FLEX ASSEMBLY
   PLASTICS
   AND TO HAVE INCORPORATED REVISED STANDARDS IN THE INCENTIVE SCHEME SO THAT THE MAXIMUM BONUS EARNINGS ARE NOT GREATER THAN 150%.

3. TO HAVE ESTABLISHED A PLAN BASED UPON THE USE OF V.F.P. FOR CONTROLLING AND IMPROVING THE PERFORMANCE OF THE FOLLOWING INDIRECT OPERATORS:
   SETTER
   INSPECTORS
   LABOURERS
   STOREKEEPERS.

4. TO HAVE ESTABLISHED A SOUND MEASUREMENT OF MACHINE SERVICEABILITY, UTILISATION AND EFFICIENCY, FOR THE FOLLOWING MACHINE GROUPS:
   FLEX WIRE WINDING MACHINES
   DIE CASTING MACHINES
   MACHINE SHOP.

5. TO HAVE APPLIED VALUE ANALYSIS TO:
   THROTTLE & CHOKE CONTROLS
   BRAIDED PIPES
   (AIM: AVERAGE MATERIAL SAVINGS TO BE NOT LESS THAN 5%).

II. FACTORY COSTS & PROFITABILITY

6. "FAILURE COSTS" (i.e. scrap, rework and customer returns) are averaging £1,550 per week and at the present time preventative measures are having little effect towards reducing this figure.

6. TO HAVE REDUCED THE QUALITY FAILURE COSTS (i.e. SCRAP, REWORK, etc.) FROM THE CURRENT AVERAGE OF APPROXIMATELY £1,550 PER WEEK TO NOT MORE THAN £1,250 PER WEEK.

OBJECTIVE 6.   TO HAVE REDUCED THE QUALITY FAILURE COSTS
(i.e. scrap, rework, customer returns)
FROM THE CURRENT AVERAGE OF APPROXIMATELY
£1,550 PER WEEK TO NOT MORE THAN £1,250 PER
WEEK BY AUGUST 1967.

EXHIBIT 18

	ACTION CO-ORDINATOR — A.R.	
BREAKDOWN OF THE ACTION REQUIRED TO ACHIEVE THE OBJECTIVE	*BY WHOM*	*HAS THE ACTION BEEN DISCUSSED & AGREED?*
6 a. To organise a study & analysis of current 'quality failure' costs so as to highlight the products or processes upon which to concentrate efforts.	A. R. R. W.	
6 b. To assess, in conjunction with the Chief Production Engineer, Chief Inspector, appropriate supervision & design engineer the priority problem areas, the potential savings & the broad outline of the solution.	.A. R.	
6 c. To organise appropriate teams or individuals & to allocate each problem area to such a team for solution with a target date for completion.	A. R.	
6 d. To institute regular progress meetings with the action teams & to take corrective action where planned improvements are not being achieved.	A. R.	
6 e. To implement wire spooling & eliminate 'D' packs on flex inners in order to reduce scrap.	AJT	Yes, at initial Job Review.
6 f. To give the Chief Inspector authority to halt a process producing excessive scrap.	GCM R. W.	Yes, at initial review of R. W.
6 g. To institute regular quality review meetings to provoke corrective action on persistent poor quality from suppliers.	A. R. R. W. W. M.	Yes, at initial review of R. W.
h. To set up the facilities for carrying out process capability studies on all major items of production plant.	AJT	

TENTATIVE PROGRAMME — OBJECTIVE 6

Action Item	1966					1967							
	Aug.	Sept.	Oct.	Nov.	Dec.	Jan.	Feb.	Mar.	Apr.	May	Jun.	Jul.	
6 a.	▓	▓	▓										
6 b.				▓									
6 c.					▓	▓	▓	▓	▓	▓	▓		
6 d.					▓	▓	▓	▓	▓	▓			
6 e.						▓	▓	▓					
6 f.	▓												
6 g.	▓												
6 h.					▓	▓	▓	▓	▓	▓	▓	▓	

EXHIBIT 19

LIKELY KEY AREAS IN A MANUFACTURING PLANT

1. **Level of factory activity.**

    Product mix/range.
    Production facilities mix.

2. **Recovery of Overheads.**

    Appropriateness of expense budgets.
    Accurary of budgets.
    Recovery of Tool Costs.

3. **Product Costs.**

    Manufacturing methods.
    Excess manufacturing costs.
    Accuracy of transfer prices.
    Material Yield.
    Material Costs.
    Product profit margins.
    Competitiveness of products.

4. **Labour Productivity.**

    Productivity agreements.
    Direct labour performance.
    Indirect labour performance.
    Training of direct labour.
    Training of indirect labour.

5. **Utilisation of Current Assets.**

    Stocks of materials.
    Level of Work in Progress.
    Stocks of finished goods.

6. **Utilisation of Fixed Assets.**

    Utilisation of floor space, buildings.
    Utilisation of machines.
    Control of capital expenditure.
    Plant layout.

7. **Achievement of Acceptable Quality.**

    Quality of design.
    Quality of production.
    Scrap and rework levels.
    Returns from customers.
    Quality of bought-out materials and components.

8. **Achievement of Programme.**

    Stability of manufacturing programme.
    Machine and labour loading.
    Work planning & scheduling.

9. **Manager Performance.**

    Organisation and procedures.
    Training and development of subordinates.
    Technical staff performance.

10. **Introduction of New Products and Processes.**

    Development of new products.
    Introduction of new processes.

11. **Industrial Relations.**

    Conditions of employment.
    Wages systems and administration.
    Working conditions.
    Negotiating procedures and joint consultation.
    Absenteeism, sickness, etc.

APPENDIX I

SETTING COMPANY OBJECTIVES: BASIC FACTS: A CHECK LIST

APPENDIX II

SETTING COMPANY OBJECTIVES: INTERPRETATION: A CHECK LIST

SETTING COMPANY OBJECTIVES
BASIC FACTS—A CHECK LIST

BASIC FACTS—A CHECK LIST.

These questions are illustrative, not comprehensive.

Company performance.

Calculate key ratios: present, last 5 year trend + any forecasts.

e.g. Profit (before tax and depreciation) as

> % of sales.
> % of total expenditure.
> % of added value (i.e. sales less cost of materials).
> % of total assets employed.
> % of fixed assets (gross *and* net).
> Current assets to current liabilities.
> Liquid assets to current liabilities.
> Sales to product stocks.
> Debtors to sales.
> Materials as % of total expenditure.
> Labour as % of total expenditure.
> Services as % of total expenditure.

Present capital structure.

Forecast capital requirements.

External Environment.

Population changes and trends in major markets.

e.g. "By 1977 two thirds of the United States population will be under 35 years of age."

Changes in pattern of income groups and discretionary spending.

e.g. "Personal expenditure is rising at an average rate of 2¾% per annum in Britain. The social/income structure is moving to a diamond rather than a pyramid shape indicating a growing mass market. Proportion of personal expenditure is likely to grow in leisure and recreation goods and services; owner occupied housing; motor cars... etc."

178

Changes arising from government policy

e.g. — to build more schools;
— to nationalise certain industries;
— to develop poor regions.

Changes in technology and innovation

e.g. — impact of the development of the transistor on valve manufacturers;
— harnessing natural gas from the North Sea and its impact on other suppliers of energy.

Product/Market.

e.g. present position—last 5 years and forward expectation for *each major product and service.*

Product	Turn-over	Profit	% Profit to Turn-over	Assets employed	% Turn-over to Assets	Manage-ment resources employed	Diagnosis & Comment

Share of total market.

Competitive position—relative standing, profit performance, likely prospects.

Performance in specific markets/territories/countries and in relation to numbers and size of customers.

Stability of performance—are there significant high and low peaks during the year?
— is there a longer cyclical pattern?

Major known factors likely to affect product pricing policy.

Vulnerability in terms of technological change, obsolescence, dependence on a few large customers.

Channels of distribution.

Plans for developing the product/service.

Also: analyse the present position and plans for planned *new* products/services.

13

Physical resources.

e.g. Production facilities

  — capacity being utilized;
  — flexibility of equipment and factories—what range of products could be made;
  — age and technical quality of equipment;
  — maintenance effectiveness;
  — design methods;
  — estimating and planning methods;
  — known constraints on better production performance.

List important raw material, sources and vulnerability of supply. Who co-ordinates purchasing?

Transport pattern and costs.

Innovation.

e.g. Success of major R and D projects over last five years compared with original statement of expectations. Ratio between R and D expenditure and rate of availability of exploitation capital.

"Decay rate" of main product groups—how long would they remain on the market if innovation ceased? Analysis of present projects (new products, new or improved processes, fundamental studies; customer service etc.) in terms of

  — stated purpose;
  — time span for completion;
  — financial and human resources;
  — current view of benefits e.g. likely new products for commercial use in X years;
  — progress made towards achieving the benefits.

Major patents and dependency on these.

Revenue from royalties.

Need for licences.

Forecast research expenditure for next X years in terms of offensive research (i.e. improved or new products), defensive research (i.e. maintaining commercial position in existing products), service to production and sales.

Organisation and management development.

e.g. Present organisation structure.

Set of existing job descriptions.

Management jobs to be filled or made redundant in next five years by retirement or planned expansion or contraction.

Pattern of control information: financial and non-financial.

Analysis of qualifications/knowledge of the management group and any "gaps".

Present arrangements for recruitment, selection, setting individual objectives, appraisal, training, promotion and salary.

Worker performance.

e.g. Wages in relation to output and changes in productivity. Breakdown of categories of skilled, semi-skilled and unskilled workers.

Trends in % overtime to basic hours.

% labour costs in relation to selling price; to unit cost.

Analysis of current Trade Union agreements and a statement of common difficulties they are causing. Lost time due to accidents.

Time taken to train key workers to experienced worker standard.

Training costs.

SETTING COMPANY OBJECTIVES
INTERPRETATION—A CHECK LIST

INTERPRETATION—A CHECK LIST

These questions are illustrative, not comprehensive.

Company performance.

How do our key ratios compare with the industry average and our main competitors?

Even if they compare favourably, are *we* satisfied with them?

Does our return on assets make it likely that we will be able to attract the amount of capital we will need, when we need it, at a sensible price?

Is our capital structure sound?

Is the cash flow position satisfactory next year? the next five years?

External environment.

Are there important gaps in our understanding of these external factors which should be filled by further research?

What are the striking threats and opportunities likely to arise short term? long term?

Product/Market.

In relation to main products and services:

Is the market increasing or decreasing overall and what is the trend of our share of it?

Is this trend something we can tie up with a trend in the external environment e.g. population growth, rise in Gross National Product etc?

Who really *is* the customer? i.e. do we know who makes the final decision to buy?

Do we know *why* the customer buys our product and not someone else's? i.e. what satisfaction/service/distinctive end-use does our product provide? What would the customer see as the "real value for money" he gets from it?

183

Are we highly dependent on a few customers?

Where is the product bought? Are we using the right distributive channels?

Who are our main competitors? Can we assess their strengths and weaknesses compared with ours?

Have we attempted to establish price-volume relationships for each product?

Are there any new competitors threatening—directly? and indirectly in providing other ways to satisfy our customers' basic needs?

How effective is our present sales organisation? When did we last review territories? What is the trend of selling expenses to turnover? to salesman? to sales? Why is the average order value decreasing? Why is the success ratio on tenders submitted declining? Are our agents effective? Are we getting the best advice and service we could from our advertising agents?

Does our product range form a logical pattern?

Is our price structure competitive and logical?

Is there scope for developing

— present products in present markets?
— new products in present markets?
— current products in new markets?
— new products in new markets?

Will an attempt to group main products under Drucker's breakdown (56) help us to rank them and suggest action:

Tomorrow's breadwinners—new products or today's bread-winners modified and improved (rarely today's bread-winners unchanged).

Today's breadwinners—the innovations of yesterday.

Products capable of becoming net contributors if something drastic is done; e.g., converting a good many buyers of "special" variations of limited utility into customers for a new, massive "regular" line. (This is the in-between category.)

Yesterday's breadwinners—typically products with high volume, but badly fragmented into "specials", small orders, and the like, and requiring such massive support as to eat up all they earn, and plenty more.

Yet this is—next to the category following—the product class to which the largest and best resources are usually allocated. ("Defensive research" is a common example.)

The "also rans"—typically the high hopes of yesterday that, while they did not work out well, nevertheless did not become outright failures. These are always minus contributors, and practically never become successes no matter how much is poured into them. Yet there is usually far too much managerial and technical ego involved in them to drop them.

The failures—these rarely are a real problem as they tend to liquidate themselves.

Physical resources.

Is there under-utilisation of resources? if so, what is its scale and time pattern?

Is there a shortage of plant or equipment which is holding back profitable sales?

How do such measures of efficiency as machine utilisation, labour utilisation, maintenance costs per unit of product compare with outside standards?

Are we making full use of techniques such as work study, value analysis, network analysis to improve our efficiency?

Are we satisfied with product design in terms of ease of manufacture?

Do we have satisfactory quality specifications? Are we trying to build too much quality into our plant and products? or not enough?

How accurate is our estimating and planning?

Is there scope for standardisation of product etc.?

Is the yield on our materials satisfactory?

Is the method of purchase of materials satisfactory?

How does our production unit rank in broad technical efficiency with the best of our competitors? with the best in the world?

Innovation.

Is there evidence of a widespread wish by managers to improve the present business in every way? what examples have we?

Is our R and D programme commercially oriented and tied in with our business objectives?

Are we systematically appraising technological advances to see what improvements can be made to our processes and products? to develop new products? to identify long term threats and opportunities?

Do we know enough about the computer as a management tool?

Are we doing R and D ourselves which it would be better to sub-contract?

What plans do we have to fill the revenue gap which will arise when our major patents expire?

Organisation and management development.

Are there clear statements of company and unit objectives and results expected?

Is responsibility delegated in a way which encourages a clear accountability for results?

Do individual managers have clear statements of what results they must produce, with appropriate standards of performance and time limits?

Is the line of command clear?

Are the techniques of control soundly linked with results expected, so that "management by exception" is possible?

What is the range and depth of knowledge/expertise in our management group? are we using it fruitfully? are there serious gaps we should fill, especially looking to the future?

Is there a regular review of each manager's performance and an assessment of his future potential?

Are training plans built up systematically from proven manager needs or developed in isolation by the training department?

186

Do we have a realistic succession plan? are there any worrying gaps we should try to fill?

Does our salary and promotion structure really attract and reward the outstanding performers?

Is a sense of commitment, drive to get results and entrepreneurial vitality widespread? or do we find it difficult to fill the tough jobs and struggle against complacency, bureaucracy and "playing it safe"?

Worker performance.

Is the productivity of labour increasing? If not, whose fault is it?

How do such indices as labour turnover, absenteeism, accident lost time, hours lost through disputes compare with the industry average? with the best of our competitors?

Are labour relations satisfactory in more subjective terms— co-operation in introducing new methods—changes in restrictive practice; quality of contribution at consultative meetings; frankness of discussion with union leaders?

Are we satisfied with the *basic principles* underlying our wage methods and setting of levels for differentials and conditions of employment? Are we spending time and money on patching up a fabric which is obsolete?

What plans must we develop to take the initiative in improving fundamentally our worker performance and attitude in the next five years?

Is our investment in training and retraining adequate?

Is the proportion of skilled to non-skilled satisfactory for the future? Are there new skills we ought to be creating?

Are our training methods effective? do people learn their jobs by exposure when skills analysis could reduce training time between half and a third?

REFERENCES

1. SELZNIK, Phillip. Leadership in Administration.
   Row, Peterson & Co., Evanston, Illinois. 1957.

2. LEVITT, T. Marketing Myopia.
   Harvard Business Review, July-August 1960. P. 45.

3. POLITICAL AND ECONOMIC PLANNING. Thrusters and Sleepers.
   London: Allen & Unwin, 1965. 295 pp.

4. SCHAFFER, Robert H. Managing by Total Objectives.
   New York: American Management Association, 1964. 11 pp.
   (Management Bulletin 52).

5. OWEN, D. E. P. Setting Objectives.
   The Chartered Mechanical Engineer, London, September 1966.

6. THE HIERARCHY OF OBJECTIVES by Charles H. Granger.
   Harvard Business Review, May-June 1964, pp. 63-74.

7. *Ibid.*, 2.

8. OWEN, G. Planning for Profit in Research.
   Financial Times, London, 9th June 1966.

9. ANSOFF, H. Igor. Corporate Strategy.
   New York: McGraw-Hill, 1965, p, 38/39.

10. DRUCKER, Peter F. The Practice of Management.
    London: Heinemann, 1955. VII, 355 pp.

11. URWICK, ORR & PARTNERS LTD., London.

12. MACE, and MONTGOMERY, Management Problems of Corporate Acquisition.
    Division of Research, Harvard Business School, 1962.

13. *Ibid.*, 5.

14. URWICK, ORR & PARTNERS LTD., London.

15. THACKRAY, John. Singer's Saving Stitch in Time.
    Management Today, London, June 1966.

16. McGREGOR, Douglas. The Human Side of Enterprise.
    New York: McGraw-Hill, 1960. x, 246 pp.

17. HOW TO FOSTER INDIVIDUAL GROWTH by Moorhead Wright.
    The Supervisor (U.S.A.), November 1961. pp. 9-11.

18. An Unpublished Urwick, Orr & Partners Ltd. study.

19. *Ibid.*, 5.

20. SANDERS, G. S. The Management of Research Chemistry & Industry, London.

21. INSTITUTION OF WORKS MANAGERS. Spanners in the Works.
    London: The Institution (1962). 8 pp.

22. THURLEY, K. E. and HAMBLIN, A. C. The Supervisor and His Job. London: H.M.S.O., 1963. 40 pp. (D.S.I.R. Problems of Progress in Industry, No. 13).

23. MAIER, Norman R. F. and others. Superior-subordinate Communication in Management.
New York: American Management Association, 1961. 96 pp. (AMA Research Study 52).

24. *Ibid.*, 5.

25. MANAGING FOR BUSINESS EFFECTIVENESS by Peter F. Drucker.
Harvard Business Review, May-June 1963. pp. 53-60.

26. *Ibid.*, 5.

27. WHAT IS WORK? Wilfred Brown, Harvard Business Review, September/October, 1962. pp. 121/9.

28. AN UNEASY LOOK AT PERFORMANCE APPRAISAL by Douglas Mc Gregor.
Harvard Business Review, May-June 1957. pp. 89-95.

29. AN APPRAISAL OF APPRAISALS by Kay H. Rowe.
Journal of Management Studies, March 1964, Vol. 1, No. 1. pp. 1-25.

30. SPLIT ROLES IN PERFORMANCE APPRAISAL by H. Meyer, E. Kay, J. French.
Harvard Business Review, January-February 1965.

31. MOTIVATIONAL APPROACH TO MANAGEMENT DEVELOPMENT by Rensis Likert.
Harvard Business Review, July-August 1959. pp. 75-82.

32. *Ibid.*, 26.

33. HOW TO IMPROVE EXECUTIVE TRAINING. Interview with Lyndall F. Urwick.
Nation's Business, July 1958.

34. MEASURES IN THE MAKING OF MANAGERS by Gordon F. Hird.
Engineering, 16th February 1962, pp. 236-237.

35. ORGANISATION FOR ECONOMIC CO-OPERATION AND DEVELOPMENT.
Evaluation of Supervisory and Management Training Methods.
Paris O.E.C.D., 1963. 159 pp.

36. THE EFFECT OF A SUPERVISORY TRAINING COURSE IN CHANGING SUPERVISORS' PERCEPTIONS AND EXPECTATIONS OF THE ROLE OF MANAGEMENT by A. J. M. Sykes.
Human Relations, August 1962, Vol. 15, No. 3, pp. 227-243.

37. URWICK, Lyndall F. The Value of Eccentricity.
Harvard Business School Bulletin, October 1959.

38. GENERAL ELECTRIC COMPANY. Developing Executive Skills by Harold F. Smiddy.
New York: American Management Association, 1955. 24 pp.
(General Management Series, No. 174).

39. THE GLACIER METAL COMPANY. Objectives of the Glacier Project.
Original terms of reference of the Glacier Project. Unpublished.

40. NATIONAL INDUSTRIAL CONFERENCE BOARD. Developing Managerial Competence: Changing Concepts, Emerging Practices. New York, The Conference Board, 1964. 128 pp. (Studies in Personnel Policy No. 189).

41. COLE Lord. Interview recorded in "Observer" Weekend Review, 6th January, 1963.

42. CORDINER, Ralph J. Interview recorded in International Management, November 1963.

43. *Ibid.,* 9.

44. *Ibid.,* 4.

45. Article on Marks & Spencers Ltd. Management Today, September 1966.

46. CORDINER, Ralph J. New Frontiers for Professional Managers. New York: McGraw-Hill, 1956. 121 pp.

47. YOUR JOB AND MINE-WHAT CHANGE IS DOING TO THEM by Stanley F. Teele. Harvard Business School Bulletin, August 1960. pp. 7-14.

48. INFORMATION NETWORKING by Norbert Stahl. Mechanical Engineering, December 1964. pp. 35-37.

48A. THOMSON, Sir William, 1st Baron Kelvin. Electrical Units of Measurement. In Popular Lectures and Address, 2nd ed., Vol. 1, London: Macmillan, 1891. pp. 80-143.

49. URWICK, Lyndall F. The Pattern of Management. London: Pitman, 1956. 100 pp.

50. STEINER, George and CANNON, Warren M. Multi-national Corporate Planning. The Macmillan Company, New York, 1966.

51. *Ibid.,* 2.

52. *Ibid.,* 16.

53. WHYTE, William H. The Organization Man. London: Jonathan Cape, 1957. 429 pp.

54. WALTER, S. J. and HARLING, J. W. Simulation of the Activities of a Papermaking Group. Paper presented to Annual Conference of the British Operational Research Society, September 1966.

55. BRIDGMAN, P. T. and GREEN, J. F. Coming to Terms with Advanced Management Information Systems. Presented to the South West Regional Conference of the British Institute of Cost and Works Accountants, 1st October 1966.

56. *Ibid.,* 25.

FURTHER READING

ANSOFF, H. Igor.
Corporate strategy; an analytic approach to business policy for growth and expansion. New York, McGraw-Hill, 1965. 240 pp. Bibliog.

BISHOP, S. V.
Business planning and control. London. The General Educational Trust of the Institute of Chartered Accountants in England and Wales, 1966. 108 pp. Bibliog. (Management Information 1).

BROWN, Wilfred.
Exploration in Management. Heinemann, London 1960. 326 pp.

DIEBOLD, John.
Beyond Automation. New York, McGraw-Hill, 1964. 200 pp.

DRUCKER, Peter F.
Managing for results: economic tasks and risk-taking decisions. London, Heinemann, 1964. 224 pp. Bibliog.

DRUCKER, Peter F.
The practice of management. London, Heinemann, 1955. 355 pp.

EWING, David W. *editor*.
Long-range planning for management. Rev. ed. New York, Harper, 1964. 565 pp.

HUMBLE, J. W.
Improving management performance. London, British Institute of Management, 1965. 38 pp. Bibliog.

IRWIN, Patrick H.
How to make a profit plan. Hamilton, Ontario, The Society of Industrial and Cost Accountants of Canada, 1961. 84 pp. Bibliog.

IRISH MANAGEMENT INSTITUTE and THE ADVISORY SERVICE OF THE IRISH NATIONAL PRODUCTIVITY COMMITTEE.
Planning your business. Dublin, The Stationery Office, 1966. 84 pp.

MacCONKEY, Dale D.
How to manage by results. New York, American Management Association, 1965.

MacGREGOR, Douglas.
The human side of enterprise. New York, McGraw-Hill, 1960.

MILLER, Ernest C.
Objectives and standards: approach to planning and control. New York, American Management Association, 1966. 120 pp. (AMA Research Study 74).

NATIONAL INDUSTRIAL CONFERENCE BOARD.
Developing managerial competence: changing concepts, emerging practices. New York, The Board, 1964. 128 pp.

192

ODIORNE, G. S.
Management by objectives: a system of managerial leadership. New York, Pitman, 1965. 204 pp.

PAYNE, Bruce.
Planning for company growth: the executive's guide to effective long range planning. New York, McGraw-Hill, 1963. 316 pp.

SCHLEH, Edward, C.
Management by results: the dynamics of profitable management. New York, McGraw-Hill, 1961. 266 pp.

SCOTT, Brian W.
Long-range planning in American industry. New York, The American Management Association, 1965. 288 pp. Bibliog.

SLOAN, Alfred P.
My years with General Motors. New York, Doubleday, 1963. 472 pp.

STEINER, George A. *editor.*
Managerial long-range planning. New York, McGraw-Hill, 1963. 334 pp.

STEINER, George A. and CANNON, Warren M. *editors.*
Multi-national Corporate Planning. New York, The Macmillan Company, 1966.

Made and printed by offset in Great Britain by William Clowes and Sons, Limited
London and Beccles